TROY

TROY

AN EPIC TALE
OF RAGE, DECEPTION
AND DESTRUCTION

BEN HUBBARD

amber
BOOKS

Published by
Amber Books Ltd
United House
North Road
London
N7 9DP
United Kingdom
www.amberbooks.co.uk
Appstore: itunes.com/apps/amberbooksltd
Facebook: www.facebook.com/amberbooks
Twitter: @amberbooks

ISBN: 978-1-78274-590-7

Project Editor: Michael Spilling
Designer: Jerry Williams
Picture Research: Terry Forshaw

Printed in UAE

Contents

Introduction

Troy is perhaps the most famous city in history, the poem about the Trojan war perhaps the greatest ever written. It is how the world remembers the ten-year Greek siege and the saga of 'strife, havoc and violent death' that raged before Troy's walls.

T HE DOWNFALL of Troy is not described by Homer, author of the *Iliad*, the epic poem about the war, but the Roman poet Virgil. It is the Trojan prince Aeneas, hero of Virgil's *Aeneid*, who details the terrible slaughter of his people. Aeneas tells about the deception of the wooden horse and how the Greeks put Troy to fire and the sword. No-one found was spared, not the young, female, nor old:

Pyrrhus came on, like Achilles himself in his onset. No bolts or bars, no guards could hold off that attack. The door crumbled under the ceaseless battering. The hinge-posts were wrenched off their sockets, and fell outwards. Utmost violence opened a passage. With access forced, and the first guards cut down, the Greek army flooded in and filled all the palace with its men; more fiercely even, than some foaming river which breaks its banks and leaps over them in a swirling torrent and defeats every barrier. – VIRGIL, *AENEID*, BOOK II

OPPOSITE: **The fall of Troy is depicted here on the fifteenth century bronze doors of Castel Nuovo, Naples.**

ABOVE: A rendering of
Troy being sacked by
the Mycenaeans is
shown in this seventeenth
century painting by
Jean Maublanc.

The legendary city of Troy, a once great trading centre of splendour and sophistication, was destroyed by war some time in the thirteenth century BCE. For centuries afterwards, the ruined stone and rubble of this city lay buried with the secret of its fate. There has seldom been a more complicated archaeological pile than the mound known as Hisarlik in Turkey. Here, where experts agree Homer's Troy lies, are buried not one but nine different cities. The hill contains skeletons, heaps of sling missiles and evidence of fire and violent destruction. Troy was a city that tried to defend itself, but was in the end overrun. Does this mean the stories of Homer and Virgil were true?

The archaeologists set out to prove they were; that a coalition of Greeks had sailed to the city to take back Helen, estranged wife of Menelaus of Sparta. But Troy's walls could not be breached and the Greeks besieged the city for ten years before winning it by trickery. Helen, slaves, plunder and vengeance were the prizes.

The first man to dig for the truth was nineteenth century millionaire, Heinrich Schliemann. Schliemann was a fantasist who falsified evidence to fit the myth of Troy. His approach at the dig site was brutal. In his rush to discover the city, Schliemann cut a deep swathe through the centre of Hisarlik, destroying large chunks of evidence in the process. The amateur archeologist partly redeemed himself, however, when he unearthed the tombs of the warrior kings who ruled at Mycenae.

Glory and Treasure

The warriors of the *Iliad* belonged to a great age of heroes, when the superpowers of the Bronze Age were led by battle-hungry aristocrats bent on glory and treasure. Homer describes the complications of this warrior code: there is pig-headed Agamemnon, king of the Greeks; there is the coward who caused all the trouble, the prince Paris; there are Hector and Achilles, the supreme warriors doomed to die.

BELOW: **This bronze Corinthian helmet dates from around 500 BCE.**

No one is a match for Achilles in war, but his rage and his self-centredness cost the lives of 'countless' numbers of his comrades. Achilles refuses to continue fighting when his leader Agamemnon takes from him Briseis, a female slave won in battle. He sulks in his tent while the Greeks are slaughtered. The use of women as commodities is one of the central motifs of Troy; the capture of female slaves as booty the reality of Bronze Age war.

The great Mycenaean city-states were wholly dependent on a workforce of slaves. The Mycenaean warriors were predatory raiders who attacked Aegean settlements and took captives as forced labour. Much treasure was needed to support the lifestyles of the palace nobles; being a 'sacker of cities' was a title of honour among them. Tablets found at the palace of Pylos list hundreds of women snatched from Anatolian shores. Some have wondered if the *Iliad*'s Helen was simply a metaphor for the many slave women taken from Troy.

To bribe Achilles back into the siege at Troy, Agamemnon offers Achilles 'twenty Trojan women, the loveliest after Helen herself.' The extent of Achilles' interest in female sex slaves, however, remains in dispute. It is the death in battle of his beloved Patroclus that persuades Achilles to return to the fight. When he hears Patroclus has been slain, Achilles wails inconsolably and throws himself over the corpse. This gesture was usually reserved for the wives of fallen husbands, and many Greeks believed that Achilles and Patroclus were not only brothers-in-arms, but also lovers.

Love Between Men

Ancient Greece had a long tradition of acceptance and even celebration of male homosexuality. Some city-states practised an elaborate code of pederasty, or sexual relationships between a man and a boy. The Theban Sacred Band was a formidable fighting elite made solely of homosexual couples; the Greek historian Plutarch was a great advocate of this model's effectiveness in war.

The Theban Sacred Band was a formidable fighting elite made up solely of homosexual couples.

In a blind rage, Achilles sets out to avenge the death of Patroclus, a period of wanton slaughter that ends with the slaying of the Trojan prince, Hector. Achilles cuts holes in Hector's ankles so he can drag his body around the walls of Troy by chariot. Such is the characteristic brutality of the *Iliad*. Homer is a virtuoso of literary violence. His warriors are graphically maimed and slain, their skulls split and their eyeballs popped, their teeth shattered by spears and their severed heads rolling in the dust while 'yet speaking'. However, alongside the brutality is pathos, as Homer gives each fallen warrior a name and a biography. The terrible human cost of war is never forgotten.

In the historical world, however, those who fell in the great Bronze Age collapse remain largely faceless and nameless. At this time, the great city-states of the Mediterranean and the Near East were attacked by earthquakes, famine and barbarians. As a dark age descended, the symbols of civilization were lost: trade, diplomacy and literacy. When the Greeks re-emerged from the dark they had to reinvent themselves and their alphabet. A great Greek poet probably used it to create the *Iliad*. And with it, the story of Troy became part of history.

THE CHARACTERS OF TROY

THE CHARACTERS OF the *Iliad*, the *Odyssey* and the *Aeneid* are central to this book. A short biography of each follows:

THE GREEKS

Achilles
Born of the goddess Thetis, Achilles is the greatest Greek warrior. He slays the Trojan champion Hector, after sulking for much of the war.

Agamemnon
King of Mycenae and leader of the Greeks, his clash of egos with Achilles nearly costs him the war.

Helen
Princess of Sparta and daughter of Zeus, Helen is the most beautiful woman in the world, and her abduction leads to the war.

Patroclus
Achilles' closest comrade in arms and presumed lover, Patroclus' death sparks Achilles' return to war.

Menelaus
Helen's husband and Agamemnon's brother; it is partly to save Menelaus' honour that the war in Troy is launched.

Odysseus
King of Ithaca and architect of the wooden horse, he is the hero of the *Odyssey*, the sequel to the *Iliad* and the tale of Odysseus's journey home after the fall of Troy.

THE TROJANS

Hector
Second in war only to Achilles, Hector is the son of Priam, king of Troy.

Priam
The great leader of the fabled city, Priam is doomed to die because of his son Paris's folly.

Paris
Vain and cowardly, Paris is a womanizer who prefers the bedroom to the battlefield.

Aeneas
Warrior and leader of the survivors of Troy, Aeneas will lead them to found the new civilization of Rome.

THE GODS

Zeus
King of the Gods, who sides with the Trojans and then the Greeks, after striking a deal with his wife, Hera.

Hera
The wife of Zeus and hater of the Trojans after Paris declares Aphrodite, and not her, winner of a beauty contest.

Apollo
Son of Zeus and champion of the Trojans, Apollo brings a plague upon the Greeks for disrespecting his priest, Chryses.

Athena
Champion of the Greeks, Athena helps break the truce between the two armies by appearing as a mortal and injuring Menelaus so the fighting will resume.

Aphrodite
Goddess of love and champion of the Trojans, Aphrodite offers Helen to Paris.

CHAPTER 1

The City of Troy

Troy has haunted the world's imagination for 3000 years. There is no more famous tale than that of Achilles and Agamemnon, the Trojan Horse, the great city itself and Helen, 'the face that launched a thousand ships/And burnt the topless towers of Ilium'.

T ROY, or Ilium as Christopher Marlowe calls it above, is portrayed by Homer as a city of great splendour and sophistication. Protected by huge limestone walls and towers, Troy sits high on its rocky prominence like a mounted jewel, a coastal beacon that flashes across the windswept Anatolian plain below and the wine-dark Aegean beyond.

It is to the city that Helen is brought – either willingly as the seduced woman, or by force – by Paris, son of King Priam of Troy. This insult to the honour of Helen's husband, King Menelaus, sparks the massive Greek expedition to the shores of Troy. Here, as the siege unfolds over ten years, the coalition boils and seethes and threatens to tear itself to pieces; the Greek heroes snarl at one another and snap over the spoils, from this war and others past.

For many of the warriors, loot is the main payoff in a conflict whose purpose is often in dispute. Over time, the lives of the

OPPOSITE: The ancient ruins of Troy, excavated from the mound of Hisarlik in modern-day Turkey.

common soldiers encamped in their makeshift beachfront huts becomes squalid. During the day, they are caught in a stalemate of attack and retreat on the battlefield plain before them. At night, they return to rest on beds made of animal skins as wild dogs feed on the carcasses of the fallen. Here, the still battlefield becomes a dark wasteland of 'corpses, abandoned weapons and black blood.' Standing behind the Greek soldiers are their ships, ready to transport them back to home and family; except the sails and timbers have long since rotted.

Internal Divisions

While the Greek soldiers remain largely loyal and faceless, their storied leaders are murderously divided. At the start of the *Iliad*, the supreme Greek leader, King Agamemnon of Mycenae, has a violent argument with the greatest Greek warrior, Achilles, over a woman taken as a trophy of war by Achilles.

The argument between the two heroes quickly becomes brutal, personal and undignified. Achilles accuses Agamemnon of greed and cowardice. He calls him a drunkard 'with the eyes of a dog, steeped in insolence and lust of gain.' The great king, he

BELOW: This artist's rendering of the city of Troy during the Bronze Age suggests an all-out assualt on the city's high walls would have been an unrealistic strategy.

says, is more interested in loot than in fighting – a deadly insult according to the terms of the warrior code.

Agamemnon in turn accuses Achilles of arrogance and sedition and invites him to return to Greece. 'There is no king here so hateful to me as you are, for you are ever quarrelsome and ill-affected…go home, then, with your ships and comrades.'

As the anger and uncertainty mounts, their supposed prize, Helen, sits protected in the high citadel of Troy. Here, she weaves a crimson blanket that tells the tale being played out in her honour. The splendid city is set in brutal contrast with the

ABOVE: This mosaic discovered at the Roman city of Pompeii depicts Achilles and Agamemnon from the *Iliad*.

ABOVE: **An artwork showing the famous walls of Troy from the north. According to legend, only trickery could bring about the city's fall.**

undignified scrap among the Greek soldiers in their makeshift camp. Troy is calm, stable and concerns itself with family life, even during warfare. Inside there is luxury, comfort and resources enough, even after ten years, to make sacrifices of twelve heifers to the gods; outside, the city's high walls show no signs of buckling before the invaders. The scene is described in the *Iliad*:

The splendid palace of King Priam, adorned with colonnades of hewn stone. In it there were fifty bedchambers – all of hewn stone – built near one another, where the sons of Priam slept, each with his wedded wife. Opposite these, on the other side of the courtyard, there were twelve upper rooms also of hewn stone for Priam's daughters, built near one another, where his sons-in-law slept with their wives. – HOMER, *ILIAD*, BOOK VI

So Homer paints the picture of the two opposing forces during the action of the *Iliad*. Here are some of the main players in the drama: Achilles, Agamemnon, Priam, Helen and the city of Troy itself. In the end it would take an act of trickery to bring about the city's downfall. The Trojan Horse, with its secret band of Greek soldiers, is a symbol so powerful that 2800 years after the famous text was written we still use it as a metaphor in everyday speech. With the horse, the siege is ended and the Greeks destroy the great city with terrible brutality.

The tale of Troy has the grandeur and apparent inevitability of tragedy. The circle of devastation now complete, Helen

THE TROJAN HORSE

PRESENTED TO THE TROJANS as an oversized goodbye offering – but in reality hiding a handful of Greek commandos ready to sow murder and ruin after nightfall – the horse is one of the most unlikely aspects of the Trojan War. Menelaus briefly recounts the story in the *Odyssey*, as it is Odysseus himself who creeps from the horse with his men and opens the gates for the freshly returning Greek ships.

It might seem inconceivable that the Trojans would be so stupid as to accept the gift. As the *Odyssey* tells us, some inside the walls of Troy also had their suspicions. Helen herself walks around the horse like an enchantress, mimicking the voices of the Greek soldiers' wives in an apparent attempt to make them give themselves away.

Can the horse be explained? One theory is that it was actually a siege engine, a type of battering ram housed in a horse-shaped structure that brought down the city gates. This would fit with Homer's picture of the Greeks as underdogs who had to resort to trickery to win the day.

Another suggestion is that the horse was merely a metaphor for an earthquake that weakened the city's defences enough for the Greeks to enter. After all, goes the theory, in ancient Greece Poseidon was the god of earthquakes who often took the symbol of a horse. There is also evidence of a devastating earthquake at the supposed site of Troy.

Perhaps it is better to remember that Homer was a poet before all else, and that his poem is a work of imagination. His story might include ancient memories of siege engines and earthquakes along with the knowledge of human treachery. The horse is then both a symbol and an evocation of ancient legend.

More prosaically, the Trojan Horse was traditionally made of wood, so it would have rotted long ago. The horse eludes the archaeologists as it continues to tantalize the historians. The horse, therefore, has to remain a mystery for now.

RIGHT: The 675 BCE Mykonos vase is the earliest object depicting the Trojan Horse. Human bones were discovered inside the vase.

travels back to Sparta as Menelaus' wife; for the Greeks, order is restored; for the Trojans, there is ruin and slaughter.

But the readers of the *Iliad*, the *Aeneid*, the *Odyssey* and the *Epic Cycle* are left with one overriding question: did any of this really happen?

Searching for Troy

With Troy, a simple question leads to ever harder and more complicated ones. But there are certainly some obvious ones: Was Helen a real person? Would a coalition of Greeks have gone to war over her elopement with a Trojan? Did Troy exist? Where was it? Could it have withstood a siege of ten years? If the war took place, who were its protagonists? Were Achilles, Agamemnon, Priam, Hector and Paris real people? And finally, was the Trojan Horse real and could the Trojans have been naïve enough to bring it within their city gates?

The answer to most of these questions is: yes, why not? After all, ancient and modern history is full of stranger stories than the legend of the Trojan War. However, there is also nothing conclusive in the evidence for mythical Troy, no clear proof that places Helen, Achilles and the horse at the heart of a decade-long siege. But an examination of the archaeology and history can provide some interesting clues.

> Schliemann was something of a huckster: a scoundrel and self-aggrandizing fantasist who falsified his evidence to fit the myth of Troy.

The Archaeologists

Archaeologists were often romantics with large imaginations. The early archaeologists who went to excavate Troy were certainly of this sort. Most were hell-bent on proving that Homer's *Iliad* was true, to show the world that the bard's tale was about history. Somehow a poem 'based on a true story' seems to have an authenticity lacking in a work of pure fancy.

One of the first and most famous of these early searchers for Homer's Troy was the nineteenth-century German businessman, Heinrich Schliemann. A self-made millionaire, Schliemann has been called 'the father of Mycenaean archaeology', and was once considered among the founding greats of archaeology itself, a science in its infancy when he first travelled to Turkey in 1868. However, despite uncovering much of the site now accepted to be the city of Troy, Schliemann is now also known as something of a huckster: a scoundrel and self-aggrandizing fantasist who falsified his evidence to fit the myth of Troy. Despite Schliemann's duplicity, he nevertheless made some of the most important discoveries known to archaeology.

Schliemann began his excavation of Hisarlik, a rubble-strewn hillock where archaeologist and colleague Frank Calvert insisted to him that Troy must be buried, in 1870. According to his diaries, Schliemann had stood in a stunned reverie at the site, a copy of the *Iliad* in hand and seeming to see the Greek army massing on the plain below. Eventually, 'darkness and violent hunger' forced Schliemann to retire for the night.

BELOW: Heinrich Schliemann overlooks his excavation, which ploughed a destructive trench through the centre of Hisarlik.

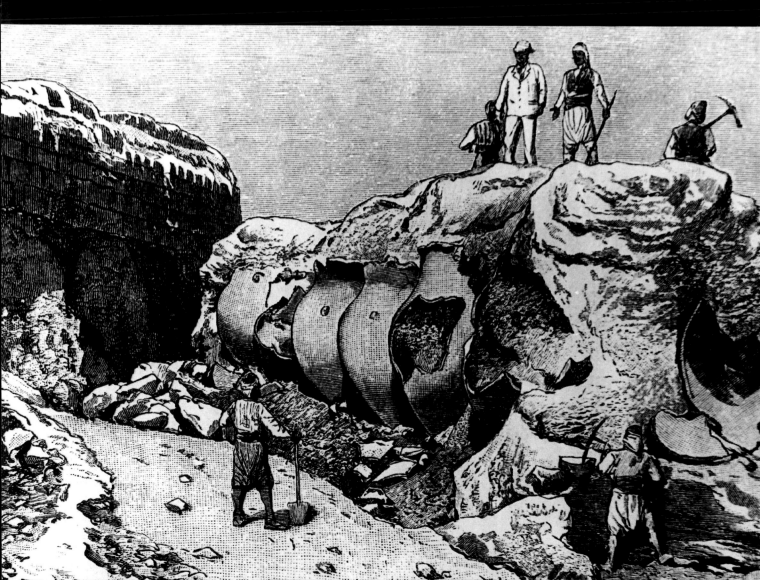

It had, Schliemann insisted, been his lifelong fantasy to find Homer's Troy, a fascination that stemmed from a boyhood image of the city given to him by his father. This seems fanciful, as Schliemann – an obsessive compiler of his own documents, which include an 11-volume autobiography, 18 travel diaries, 60,000 letters and nearly 200 volumes of excavation notes – does not mention Troy or the *Iliad* once before he retired from business aged 45.

Despite his habit of airbrushing his own history, there is no doubt that Schliemann devoted the rest of his life to the pursuit of Troy. He took to the hill of Hisarlik with ferocious gusto and a crew of 200 pickaxe-wielding men. Calvert had explained to Schliemann that there were likely to be many layers on Hisarlik and he would have to dig deep to discover the city supposedly dating from the thirteenth century BCE.

BELOW: This map drawn by Heinrich Schliemann shows what he believed to be the city of Troy as described by Homer.

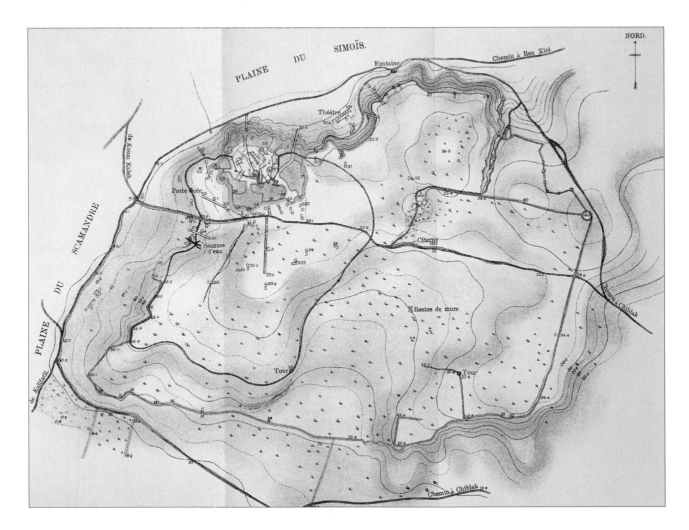

LEFT: **Part of the ancient road through Troy. Schliemann took the road as proof of the *Iliad*'s authenticity, as it was wide enough to accommodate a chariot.**

Schliemann's crew ploughed fast and furiously into Hisarlik, cutting a 14m (46ft) deep trench through the middle of the hill and destroying many precious archaeological treasures in the process. What the crew uncovered within the fifty or so layers of Hisarlik was not one but several cities built on top of the other. Near the bottom, the city later known as Troy II appeared wildly promising. Here were walls and a wide paved road that could accommodate two chariots side by side: it seemed straight out of Homer. More tantalizingly still, Schliemann found evidence of fire scorching the walls, leading him to dub Troy II the 'Burnt City'. Could this be the remains of the fire the Greeks set in Troy to raze the city to the ground?

International Stir

Schliemann's find caused a small tremor in the world of archaeology and classical studies. For centuries, Homer's Troy had been dismissed as a fairy story, a long-distant tale told by a long-dead bard. Now it seemed a real city. Look, boasted the businessman with a sort of proprietorial air, at these 'great walls'. Beneath the clouds of legend sat a rock of hard fact.

But what proof had Schliemann found? The answer, apart from scorched walls and great mounds of rubble and earth, was

ABOVE: Sophia Schliemann bedecked in the 'Jewels of Helen' which, after being photographed, were smuggled out of Turkey in a crate.

very little. The naysayers back in Europe were quick to denounce 'Homer's City' as 'Homer's Pigsty', and even Schliemann himself began to wonder. He needed something concrete, and quickly.

Whether out of coincidence or necessity, Schliemann's moment arrived in 1873. Then he presented to the world one of the greatest discoveries in archaeological history – a cache of precious objects that he called 'Priam's treasure'. Schliemann claimed he had found the hoard – gold, bronze and silver weapons and jewellery – with his teenaged wife Sophia one eventful morning. Sophia had gathered many of the smaller items, including rings, bracelets and a diadem, in her apron and carried them back to their house for further inspection. Sophia was famously bedecked and photographed in the jewellery – subsequently dubbed the 'Jewels of Helen' – before it was smuggled out of Turkey in a crate to Schliemann's palatial home in Athens.

The find set the scholarly world ablaze and captured the popular imagination. But the whole business was suspect. For one thing, Sophia had not been on the site at the time of the discovery, but with her family in Athens. It also emerged that the hoard had not been discovered all at once. Instead, evidence pointed to a series of smaller finds over the digging season, which Schliemann had put together as a glittering job lot. The 'Priam's treasure' tag brought priceless publicity, but it was wrong. The treasure was actually found to date from around 2300 BCE: 1000 years too early for Homer's Troy. Troy II, therefore, could not be the mythical city.

Schliemann had had his doubts privately. Troy II was little more than a citadel 100 metres square (1076 square ft); too small to be the grand city of the Trojan War. The disappointment was intensified by the exhausting task of the dig itself. Malaria, scorpions and biting insects combined with unceasing wind, dust and unrelenting heat often left Schliemann too sick and depressed to oversee the excavation.

There were also problems with the authorities. Schliemann had previously ignored the need for an excavation permit and now the Ottoman government was furious at the theft of its national treasures. A lawsuit ensued. Schliemann would later heal this rift with a sizeable donation. However, he broke his promises to split any findings with the government and not to damage existing structures. This led to great trouble for all archaeologists who followed Schliemann to Hisarlik.

WHERE IS TROY?

THE REMAINS OF THE city believed to be Troy are situated on a northeastern corner of the Mediterranean in what is modern Turkey. Troy would have commanded a strategic point at the southern entrance to the Dardanelles, a narrow strait that links the Black and Aegean Seas via the Sea of Marmara.

Positioned between the Scamander and Simois Rivers (today called Menderes and Dumrek Su), Troy overlooked a large Bronze Age bay that has since silted over and become farmland. This is the Troad, 'The Land of Troy'. Troy's location on the trading route between the civilizations of the Mediterranean and those in the east would have made it an important commercial centre as well as a natural stopping-off point for merchants on their voyages through the Dardanelles or the Hellespont, as the strait was known to antiquity.

An aerial view of Hisarlik with the Troad and Dardanelles in the background.

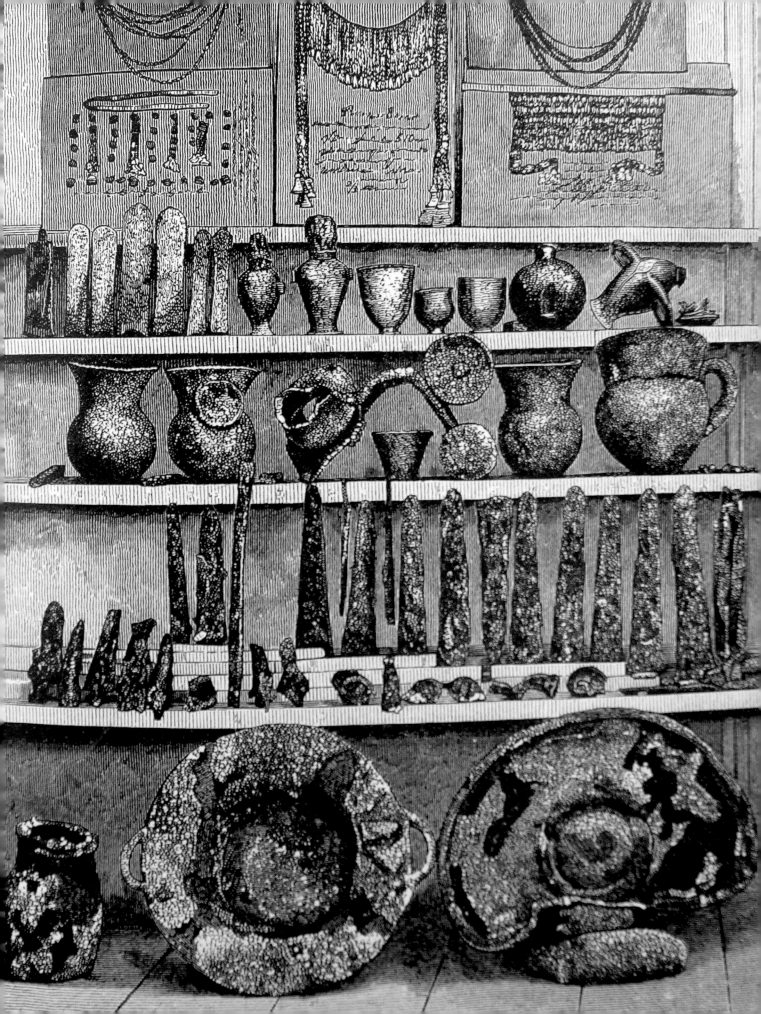

Mycenae

While waiting for the furore to pass, Schliemann turned to the Greek side of Homer's story. If Troy indeed existed, then so must have the Greeks who attacked it. The natural starting point therefore must be the grand palace of Mycenae, where Menelaus had supposedly pleaded with his brother, King Agamemnon, to help recapture his estranged wife.

Mycenae had been deserted for 2000 years by the time Schliemann reached it in 1874. Located in the Peloponnese on mainland Greece, the citadel of Mycenae commanded a lofty position between the mountains of Hagios Elias and Zara and the plain of Argos stretching out below. To Schliemann, the city seemed as Homer had described, 'broad-streeted and golden'. The citadel beyond the city's grand Lion Gate certainly seemed a worthy resting place for Agamemnon, who, according to the story, was famously murdered by his wife Clytemnestra and her lover Aegisthus when he got home from Troy.

For Schliemann to find Agamemnon's tomb would be to confirm that the ancient king existed and bring the Homeric age of heroes to life. In the late summer of 1876, this is exactly what Schliemann did.

Schliemann was not the first archaeologist to dig at Mycenae, but he was the first to excavate inside the citadel. Within a few metres, he hit paydirt. The first objects to appear were upright stone grave monuments, some of them bearing the carved images of warriors in chariots. But the best was to come: rectangular grave shafts containing the remains of 19 adults and two children, every one of them covered in gold. Fitted over the men's faces were portrait-type masks beaten from thinly hammered gold; on their

OPPOSITE: Schliemann claimed that this cache of precious objects, which he dubbed 'Priam's treasure', had been unearthed one evening with his wife Sophia. This turned out to be a lie.

BELOW: Here, an illustrator offers an interpretation of the Schliemanns discovering Trojan treasures at Hisarlik.

ABOVE: One of the beaten gold death masks unearthed at the shaft graves at Mycenae.

chests were gold rosettes and sunburst decorations. The women wore diadems on their heads, and all around the adults lay bronze swords and daggers, their hilts and scabbards depicting scenes of hunting and battle. There was more besides in this splendid hoard: silver and gold goblets and boxes, ivory chests, and hundreds of gold discs decorated with animal motifs.

Schliemann was in no doubt that he was looking at the characters and treasures from the *Iliad*. There were too many connections for it not to be. Within the scenes hammered out in gold were the boar tusk helmets described by Homer and a depiction of the 'tower-shield' as carried by Ajax. There were even the same 'silver-studded' swords that Hector gave to Ajax. Vindicated by one of the single greatest discoveries in archaeology, Schliemann described the find in his book *Mycenae*: 'For my part, I have always firmly believed in the Trojan War; my full faith in Homer and in the tradition has never been shaken by modern

THE CITY OF TROY 27

criticism, and to this faith of mine I am indebted for the discovery of Troy and its treasure.'

Except that, once again, Schliemann was wrong. Simply, the graves were from an earlier period, perhaps not even connected with the supposed dynasty of Agamemnon at all. The proof was in the gold itself, found to date from around 1600 BCE, 400 years too early for Homer's Troy. Once again, the entrepreneur was undone by the complexities of archaeology and the problem of linking myth with fact. The more important truth, however, was that while being dazzled by the riches unearthed at Troy and Mycenae Schliemann had overlooked a far humbler but altogether more significant find that linked the two cities together: fragments of Mycenaean pottery.

Colleagues such as Frank Calvert had insisted to Schliemann that the Mycenaean pottery found at the site at Hisarlik was of great relevance to his search for Troy and should not be dismissed. However, this pottery had been found at Troy VI and VII, both cities at a much higher level than the feverishly uncovered Troy I and II. Now Schliemann realized that much of the valuable material from these upper cities had simply been thrown away. In his haste to find Troy, Schliemann had destroyed much of the evidence in front of him. Convincing himself there was still time to discover his dream, Schliemann organized another dig for 1890. But he collapsed on Christmas Day in Naples and died the following day. The first great archaeologist of the myth of Troy had been utterly defeated by its enduring mystery.

BELOW: **Wilhelm Dörpfeld, assistant and successor to Heinrich Schliemann.**

Into the Light

After Schliemann's death his work continued under his assistant, Wilhelm Dörpfeld. Like Schliemann, Dörpfeld was an incurable romantic obsessed with recovering the mythical city. However, Dörpfeld was a rather more careful archaeologist than his former boss and mentor. Trained as an architect, Dörpfeld sought to develop an overall image of the shape of Troy VI, the city that, according to the Mycenaean pottery found there, was the most likely candidate for Homer's Troy.

THE NINE CITIES OF TROY

THE SITE OF TROY is made up of nine cities that spanned more than 4000 years of history. A brief description of each is given here:

TROY I: Founded around 3000 BCE, Troy I was a small citadel containing around 20 rectangular mud-brick buildings and surrounded by a 90m (295ft) fortified wall. Its lofty location gave Troy I both a commanding strategic position and access to the sea trade routes through the Dardanelles.

TROY II: Built in around 2500 BCE, Troy II added mud-brick houses alongside its citadel to accommodate its growing population. The citadel was protected by two gates and featured large, rectangular buildings called megarons; these were the religious and political heart of the city. Troy II was probably destroyed by fire.

TROY III–V: After the destruction of Troy II, the settlement went into decline. Little is known about the cities of Troy III, IV and V, except that they became smaller, more

fortified and wholly contained within the citadel. After a time of relative isolation, a new city, Troy VI, emerged in around 1900 BCE.

TROY VI–VII: The large Bronze Age cities of Troy VI and VII were protected by great defensive walls, towers and ditches and were home to around 8000 inhabitants. The cities' economy centred on trade and home-crafts such as spinning and weaving and the manufacture of purple dye from seashells.

TROY VIII: After being abandoned around 1100 BCE, the city re-emerged in 700 BCE as Troy VIII, a Hellenistic city called Ilion. The acropolis, agora and temples were typical of Greek cities during that period.

TROY IX: Sacked by the Romans in 85 BCE, Ilion became a Roman city that was partially rebuilt by the general Sulla. The emperor Augustus later built Ilion into a large city, which survived until around 324 CE. Then Constantinople was founded and Troy fell into its final decline.

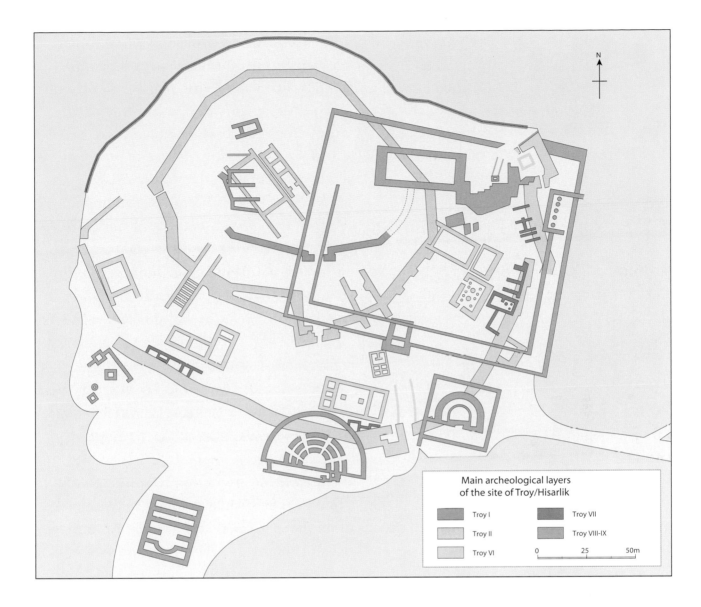

By digging around the outskirts of the settlement rather than through its middle, Dörpfeld quickly made a discovery of seemingly greater relevance to the myth of Troy than anything produced by Schliemann: magnificent, towering walls. Buried under 15m (50ft) of soil and rubble, the thick limestone walls were flanked by large watchtowers and stood 8m (26ft) high. These were of a far more sophisticated build than any of the fortifications around Mycenae. There was also compelling evidence that linked the walls with the *Iliad*: they had been built with an inward lean, or 'batter' angle, as described by Homer. Could these have been the walls that Patroclus scales nearly single-handedly in Book XVI of the *Iliad*?

ABOVE: **A map showing the nine cities of Troy.**

The sons of the Achaeans would now have taken Troy by the hands of Patroclus, for his spear flew in all directions, had not Phoebus Apollo taken his stand upon the wall to defeat his purpose and to aid the Trojans. Thrice Patroclus charged at an angle of the high wall, and thrice Apollo beat him back, striking his shield with his own immortal hands. When Patroclus was coming on like a god for yet a fourth time, Apollo shouted to him with an awful voice and said, 'Draw back, noble Patroclus, it is not your lot to sack the city of the Trojan chieftains, nor yet will it be that of Achilles who is a far better man than you are.' On hearing this, Patroclus withdrew some distance and avoided the anger of Apollo. – HOMER, *ILIAD*, BOOK XVI

ABOVE: The artwork depicted on this jug discovered at Mycenae draws heavily from the Minoan artistic style.

If the walls themselves were not proof enough for Dörpfeld, further excavations inside Troy VI revealed the remains of five large houses – each one fit for a royal resident. Within the houses, Mycenaean pottery was found scattered everywhere. There could no longer be any question of the links between Troy and the world of the Mycenae. Finally, and perhaps best of all, was evidence of great devastation at Troy VI.

For Dörpfeld, the destruction could only have been brought upon the city by a besieging army. In 1902, he wrote: 'The long dispute over the existence of Troy and over its site is at an end. The Trojans have triumphed…the countless books which in both ancient and modern times have been published against Troy have become meaningless.'

It would take another three decades for Dörpfeld's words about 'the end of the dispute' to be put in doubt. It would be the work of another archaeologist, the American Carl Blegen, to contradict Dörpfeld's notion that Troy VI was the city of the Trojan War.

Blegen began his own dig at Hisarlik in 1932. Like his predecessors, his intentions were clear: to solve the elusive mystery of Homer's Troy once and for all. His focus would be on Troy VI, the city Dörpfeld was sure had been destroyed by a great invading army. Blegen agreed that the evidence pointed to great destruction, but was less sure about what had caused it. One section of outer wall, for example, had been lifted off its foundations; other internal walls had collapsed. An army of giants or gods may have been able to rain down ruin on Troy, but it was probably not done by the men fighting for Agamemnon. Even Dörpfeld, who visited the site in 1935, was forced to agree: the damage to Troy VI had not been caused by humans but by nature: an earthquake.

While examining the evidence for an earthquake at Troy VI, Blegen came up with a new theory. Simply, he proposed that there was no cultural cut-off between the cities of Troy VI and VII: the same people had lived in both. The people from Troy VI

BELOW: **One of the great walls excavated at Hisarlik, a part of Troy VI.**

had simply built Troy VII on top of the old city and continued to occupy it.

There seemed to have been a need for rebuilding; first after the trauma of an earthquake and then later as a new foe threatened the city. Great changes had certainly taken place to the architecture of the city during the occupation of Troy VII. This had not happened gradually or carefully. This fact was most obvious in the large nobles' homes at the top of the city. These had been subdivided with roughly built walls to create more rooms. Sunken into the floors were multiple storage pots. What had been large elegant homes for single families had been quickly and roughly redesigned to accommodate a multitude. Simply put, the city had become something of a shanty town, with temporary housing thrown up for the many refugees flooding in.

But now came the most tantalizing of Blegen's theories:

THE EARTHQUAKE END

SCHLIEMANN, DÖRPFELD AND BLEGEN were all men searching for absolutes; that is, to link the fall of Troy with archaeological evidence. However, in doing so they overlooked scholarly theories that the poets' reimagining of the story had more than one factual source. The city, for example, could have fallen to an earthquake, or been weakened by an earthquake and then overrun by an army. Could the fall of Troy be a composite of several historical events? The Roman poet Virgil's classic account of the fall of Troy evokes images of great walls shaking and earth moving under the influence of the gods:

'There before my eyes I saw the dreadful vision of the gods in all their might, the enemies of Troy. At that moment I seemed to see the whole of Ilium settling into the flames and Neptune's Troy toppling over from its foundations like an ancient ash high in the mountains which farmers have hacked with blow upon blow of their double axes, labouring to fell it; again and again it threatens to fall, its foliage shudders and its head trembles and nods until at last it succumbs to its wounds and breaks with a dying groan, spreading ruin along the ridge.'

– VIRGIL, *AENEID*, BOOK II

that Troy VII was finally destroyed through warfare or, more accurately, an attacking army.

Blegen's evidence was strong on this point: spent arrowheads, unburied skeletons on the streets of the citadel, and scorch marks on the walls. Like his predecessors, Blegen felt certain of the significance of his discovery. The 'scattered remains of human bones discovered in the fire-scarred ruins of Settlement VIIA surely indicate that its destruction was accompanied by violence. Little imagination is required to see reflected here the fate of an ancient town captured and sacked by implacable foes...as is so graphically described in the accounts of marauding expeditions in the Homeric poems.'

Everything seemed to point to Troy as a city under siege with the city's residents flooding to Troy's highest point to try to escape the violence. Here they huddled in a makeshift shanty town, thrown up quickly, as the besiegers attacked the

ABOVE: The walls of Troy
VII: the evidence pointed
to a city destroyed by war.

walls below them. Then, the inevitable end; with it, slaughter,
plunder, rape and imprisonment – the fall of a city so evocatively
described by Virgil in the *Aeneid*.

Despite all that Blegen had found, there was a large hole in
his theory: the size of the city itself. As we have seen, Troy was
described as one of the great Mediterranean cities of the Bronze
Age; the walls of its own architecture confirmed to all onlookers
its ostentatious wealth. But the cities unearthed by Schliemann,
Dörpfeld and Blegen had all been disappointingly small. At only
200 by 200m (656 by 656ft) in size, Troy VII could hardly claim
to be the mighty city of Homer. Once again, the world would
require new archaeology to prove that Troy was more legend
than myth.

Troy VI and VII

And so it proved. Some 50 years after Blegen finished his dig at
Hisarlik, German archaeologist Manfred Korfmann began a new
excavation. Using the latest high-tech radiocarbon techniques,
Korfmann sought to document the sizes of Troy VI and VII and
verify how they came to an end. From the outset, Korfmann

made it clear that he was not there to investigate Homer or the Trojan War; this was a straightforward dig to learn more about a high-profile Bronze Age site.

However, he too stumbled on an irresistible piece of evidence seeming to link the city of Troy with the tale told by Homer. For Korfmann this was the discovery that the traditional Troy VI and VII made up only a small part of larger cities that stretched out deep in the earth below. He found a Troy 15 times larger than any of the previous cities, a vast settlement covering nearly 300,000 square metres (3,230,000 square ft) – a giant in Bronze Age terms.

This cleared up the mystery of Blegen's Troy, deemed too small to be a place of legend or myth. It became clear that Blegen, along with Schliemann and Dörpfeld, had been excavating only the citadel standing above a large lower city below, a common layout for late Bronze Age settlements. Furthermore, Korfmann also confirmed the existence of the Spring Cave, a network of tunnels under the city that supplied it with water.

But the most dramatic discovery was to come. In 1995, Korfmann found evidence that the lower part of Troy VII had been destroyed by fire and war. Around this area were uncovered skeletons and heaps of 'sling bullets' in an old storeroom. On further inspection, the layer beneath the storeroom, part of Troy VI, seemed clearly to have been damaged by an earthquake. The city, then, had indeed been beset by a natural disaster before a later assault by an attacking army. The jury was

BELOW: **Mother goddess statue from Troy VII, today housed in the Canakkale Archaeological Museum, Turkey.**

Apart from the fragments of pottery found during the excavations of Troy VI and VII, there is little in the archeology to link Mycenae with Troy.

BELOW: A selection of pottery discovered at Troy VI, now housed in the Istanbul Archaeology Museum.

in: Troy VII was a large, prosperous city with a population of thousands that was destroyed by war. So what, according to Korfmann, happened?

'Now the evidence is burning and catastrophe with fire,' Korfmann reported. 'Then there are skeletons, we found for example a girl, I think sixteen, seventeen years old, half buried, the feet were burned by fire. Half of the corpse was underground. This is strange so a rapid burial was in public space, inside the city, and we found sling pellets in heaps. It was a city which was besieged. It was a city which was defended, which protected itself. They lost the war and obviously they were defeated.'

Korfmann was quick to add that he could not say who had attacked Troy or why. Apart from the fragments of Mycenaean pottery found during the excavations of Troy VI and VII, there

LEFT: Manfred Korfmann, the archaeologist who made clear he was not at Hisarlik to investigate the Trojan War.

is today little in the archaeology of the site to link Mycenae with Troy at all. Carbon dating has shown that this pottery comes from the period when the Trojan War allegedly took place; some time in the thirteenth century BCE. However, it could easily be argued that the presence of this pottery makes the case for the Trojan War more remote. If Mycenae had been one of Troy's great trading partners, why would it sever a lucrative revenue stream? Would Agamemnon, the king of Mycenae, wipe out his own customers over a dispute with his brother's wife?

It is the people, therefore, who once lived among the rubble of the now excavated cities that are key to determining the validity of Homer's tale. And it is an examination of the relationship between Mycenae and Troy that is of central importance. It is these ghostly figures alongside others from antiquity – from the Egyptians to the Romans – who not only believed in the Trojan War as an actual event of world history, but were also sure where it took place and who the central players were.

It is to the civilizations of the late Bronze Age that we now turn, and the two great superpowers of the period: the Mycenaeans and the Hittites, and the warrior kings who led these peoples.

CHAPTER 2

The Warrior Kings

The great heroes of the *Iliad* are Achilles and Hector, legendary warriors honoured for their skill and courage in war. More ambiguous figures are the Greek leader Agamemnon and the Trojan prince Paris: sometimes cowardly, often vain or arrogant.

THE SUPERPOWERS of the Bronze Age were led by battle-hungry aristocrats bent on glory in war, honour and prestige among their peers, and a legacy that would outlast them. Homer's heroes are no different. However, sometimes we need to see what an unheroic warrior looks like in order to be reminded of what heroism means.

In the *Iliad*, no one is less heroic than Paris – the Trojan prince responsible for bringing the Greeks to Troy by eloping with Helen of Sparta. For his family, Paris' deed is entirely predictable. Priam, his father, admits that among his fifty sons there is a mixture of good and bad: 'I have had the bravest sons in all Troy – noble Nestor, Troilus the dauntless charioteer, and Hector...and those I am ashamed of... Liars, and light of foot, heroes of the dance, robbers of lambs and kids from your own people.'

Priam's contempt for Paris is echoed by Hector, the true hero of the *Iliad*, who says of his brother: 'Evil-hearted Paris, fair to

OPPOSITE: **A 1740 tapestry from the workshop of Jean-Francois and Pierre Van den Borght show Achilles pursuing Paris, who is protected by the goddess Aphrodite.**

see, but woman-mad, and false of tongue, would that you had never been born, or that you had died unwed. Better so, than live to be disgraced.'

Throughout the *Iliad*, it is Paris' habit to acknowledge the truth behind a telling-off: 'you have scolded me rightly, not beyond measure'. He then reminds his critic that all men are as the gods made them. Paris, or Alexandrus as he is also known, is shown as unheroic because he passively accepts his destiny as a womanizer and reluctant warrior. Yet Paris is given many opportunities to show his fighting prowess and to soften the enmity of his fellow Trojans. Paris' moment for heroism comes when the two great forces march towards each other as facing armies on the plain:

BELOW: This Greek statue of Paris dates from the first century CE.

When they were close up with one another, Alexandrus came forward as champion on the Trojan side. On his shoulders he bore the skin of a panther, his bow, and his sword, and he brandished two spears shod with bronze as a challenge to the bravest of the Achaeans to meet him in single fight. Menelaus saw him thus stride out before the ranks, and was glad as a hungry lion that lights on the carcase of some goat or horned stag, and devours it there and then, though dogs and youths set upon him. Even thus was Menelaus glad when his eyes caught sight of Alexandrus, for he deemed that now he should be revenged. He sprang from his chariot, clad in his suit of armour.

Alexandrus quailed as he saw Menelaus come forward, and shrank under cover of his men. As one who starts back affrighted, trembling and pale, when he comes suddenly upon a serpent in some mountain glade, even so did Alexandrus plunge into the throng of Trojan warriors, terror-stricken at the sight of the son of Atreus.

— HOMER, *ILIAD*, BOOK III

As Paris trembles at the sight of his formidable opponent, Hector berates him: 'Did you not from your far country carry off a lovely woman wedded among a people of warriors – to bring sorrow upon your father, your city, and your whole country, but joy to your enemies, and hang-dog shamefacedness to yourself? And now can you not dare face Menelaus and learn what manner of man he is whose wife you have stolen?'

True to type, Paris accepts the truth behind his brother's words and offers a reluctant solution:

Hector, your rebuke is just... If you would have me do battle

ABOVE: **The battle between Menelaus and Paris over Helen of Troy.**

while he and I fight in their midst for Helen and all her wealth. Let him who shall be victorious and prove to be the better man take the woman and all she has, to bear them to his home, but let the rest swear to a solemn covenant of peace whereby you Trojans shall stay here in Troy, while the others go home to Argos and the land of the Achaeans.

– HOMER, *ILIAD*, BOOK III

The Duel

So the scene is set to settle the issue of Helen by a duel between two men, not two armies. It is a moment of reprieve for the Greeks, the Trojans and the reader: will the individuals responsible for the war resolve it honourably by fighting each other and saving the bloodshed of many? Hector announces the suggestion to the Greeks, who strip off their armour and take a seat on the battlefield. Menelaus demands that Priam come down to seal the agreement with a sacrifice. Helen herself looks down from the city walls. The stage is set for a great piece of heroism, a duel to the death in the epic warrior tradition. It is not, however, fated to that end.

The duel is brief; Homer describes the scene in forty lines. It began with Paris hurling a spear at Menelaus, which strikes his shield. Menelaus then brings his 'silver-studded sword' down upon Paris' helmet, shattering it in the process. Menelaus grabs Paris by his helmet chinstrap and drags him towards the Greek lines. As Paris begins to choke, suddenly there is divine intervention: Aphrodite, Paris' patron, breaks his chinstrap and throws down a mist. This allows the goddess to whisk the Trojan away to his own bedchamber. One of his patron gods has rescued him, as other gods will rescue their pet humans throughout the poem.

The gods and fate always have ultimate power over mere humans. However, men are also seen as forging their own fate, at least within certain boundaries. This doesn't stop other men from criticizing warriors for what they do. Paris' cowardice will inflame the wrath of the Greeks until his father's city is destroyed and his prize taken.

Aphrodite tells Helen to go to Paris in his bedchamber. Here, she derides her lover: 'So you are come from the fight. Would that you had fallen rather by the hand of that brave man who was my husband. You used to brag that you were a better man with hands and spear than Menelaus. Go, and challenge him again – but I should advise you not to do so, for if you are foolish enough to meet him in single combat, you will soon fall by his spear.'

'So you are come from the fight. Would that you had fallen rather by the hand of that brave man who was my husband.'

BELOW: Helen and King Priam watch the fight between Menelaus and Paris from safety of the walls of Troy.

Meanwhile, Menelaus rages on the battlefield in a desperate search for his quarry. However, 'No man, neither of the Trojans nor of the allies, could find him. If they had seen him they were in no mind to hide him, for they all of them hated him as they did death itself.'

Menelaus calls out that he is the victor of the duel, but in reality neither party has been defeated. It is now for the gods to decide, and the deal struck between Hera and Zeus means not only the ruin of Troy, but that of the Greek cities of Argos, Sparta and Mycenae. The duel has failed; now all will feel the power of the gods to devastate and destroy.

Heroic Aristocrats

Part of the horror of Achilles' slaying of Hector is the deeply unheroic behaviour that follows. Achilles drives his spear through Hector's corpse and encourages his comrades to do the same. He then strips off the armour that Hector stole from Patroclus and cuts holes in his heels. Through these, Achilles

ACHILLES AND HECTOR

A DUEL FOUGHT BY heroic champions is one of the great motifs of the *Iliad*. None is more anticipated than that of the battle between Achilles and Hector. Here, the contradictions of honour and heroism are played out in complex detail. Achilles, a hero who has refused to fight for his king, becomes a merciless slaying machine after the death of his beloved Patroclus. Achilles had previously spared some of his victims, selling them into slavery rather than killing them. But now he butchers his way through the ranks of Trojans without pity or pause.

Hector, by comparison, shows himself as honourable in warfare and family life and a principled father and leader of men. However, it is Hector who stumbles before the final showdown with Achilles and runs in fear instead of standing to fight. A chase begins around the walls of Troy until Hector stops to face Achilles. Here he asks that the winner will treat his foe's body respectfully and return it to his family. Achilles refuses: 'You shall now pay me in full for the grief you have caused me on account of my comrades whom you have killed in battle.'

Both champions hurl their spears without result. Hector, realizing the gods are on the side of Achilles, calls out: 'My

LEFT: The epic battle between Hector and Achilles, as depicted by painter Peter Paul Rubens (1577–1640).

doom has come upon me; let me not then die ingloriously and without a struggle, but let me first do some great thing that shall be told among men hereafter.'

As Hector speaks, he: *drew the keen blade that hung so great and strong by his side, and gathering himself together he sprang on Achilles like a soaring eagle which swoops down from the clouds on to some lamb or timid hare – even so did Hector brandish his sword and spring upon Achilles. Achilles mad with rage darted towards him…the gleam of the spear which Achilles poised in his right hand [was] fraught with the death of noble Hector. He eyed his fair flesh over and over to see where he could best wound it, but all was protected by the goodly armour of which Hector had spoiled Patroclus after he had slain him, save only the throat where the collarbones divide the neck from the shoulders, and this is a most deadly place: here then did Achilles strike him as he was coming on towards him, and the point of his spear went right through the fleshy part of the neck.* – HOMER, *ILIAD*, BOOK XXII

Then Achilles dishonours the fallen warrior by denying him funeral rites and desecrating his body.

Homer, it becomes clear, not only champions the warrior code; he is also a critic of it.

BELOW: Using holes cut in his ankles, Achilles dragged Hector's body through the dust behind his chariot.

pulls the girdle that Ajax gave to Hector and attaches it to his chariot. Three times he drives around Patroclus' funeral pyre, dragging Hector's cadaver behind him in the dust. The desecration continues for twelve days, as Priam and Andromache, Hector's wife, weep inside the Trojan citadel. Achilles, the great hero of the Greeks, has in his rage betrayed the heroic code.

Homer, it becomes clear, not only champions the warrior code; he is also a critic of it. Achilles' murderous sulk following his quarrel with Agamemnon costs his fellow Greeks 'countless lives', as Homer says in the second line of the epic. The poet draws an implicit contrast between the killing machine Achilles, with no family ties and little care for the welfare of the Greeks, and the family man and great tribal leader Hector.

In a justly famous scene from Book VI, Hector embraces his wife Andromache and cuddles his infant son when he cries in fright at the waving horsehair plume on his father's helmet. In a terrible premonition of the downfall of the city, Hector says he grieves for none of the Trojans as much as for Andromache, and is glad that he will be dead rather than see an Achaean 'rob you of your freedom and bear you weeping away.'

The ideals of honour and heroism in the Bronze Age pose many dilemmas in practice. Homer's portrait of heroism centres on the kings and princes of Mycenae and Troy, great leaders of men supposedly descended from the Olympian gods. As we have seen, these warrior aristocrats were supposedly bound to certain codes of honour in war that did not always prevail in practice.

ABOVE: Here, Andromache mourns Hector after his body is retrieved from Achilles by Priam.

However, is all of this an accurate portrait of the Bronze Age kingdoms in which the *Iliad* is set? This was around 500 years before Homer composed his poem. So what was the world really like during the late Bronze Age when the Trojan War is alleged to have taken place? Who were the great superpowers that controlled world events at this time?

Mycenae

The Bronze Age world was made up of city-states ruled by warrior kings. These city-states often formed confederations or became part of large empires. In our search for Troy, it is important to examine two of these superpowers: the Mycenaeans and the Hittites of Anatolia.

Mycenae was an elite warrior culture that established itself in Greece through war and conquest. The Mycenaeans, whose

ABOVE: An aerial view of the citadel of Mycenae, protected behind its imposing Cyclopean walls.

culture resembled the Minoans, the grand civilization whose capital of Knossos lay in Crete, flourished between 1600 and 1100 BCE. Mycenaean Greece was a patchwork of city-states sharing the same religion, culture and architecture. Grand palace citadels built with thick walls for defence were the defining feature of these cities, often constructed in lofty positions to control the local populace who lived in settlements below. The largest city-states were Pylos, Tiryns and Midea in the Peloponnese; Athens, Thebes and Orchomenos in Central Greece; and Lolcos in Thessaly. However, the largest and most important city-sate was Mycenae itself.

Although settling in strongholds around the Aegean, the Mycenaeans had a reputation for being sailors, traders and raiders. They bought, bartered and sold goods when they could; when this didn't work they took what they wanted. Hittite texts, in particular, record occasions when bands of Mycenaean warriors harassed the west coast of Anatolia in their search for plunder.

It is easy to imagine Agamemnon, the great sacker of cities, attacking these settlements. Certainly, Mycenaean Greece laid the cultural foundations for the Greek world of Homer's own day and beyond. Later Greeks borrowed many of their gods from the Mycenaean pantheon; the Mycenaean language, the script known as Linear B, was the precursor of the Greek language.

Many tablets written in Linear B were found by archaeologist Carl Blegen at the citadel of Pylos, the traditional palace of Agamemnon's close ally, King Nestor. Blegen hoped the scripts would be a great retelling of the Trojan War itself, but they proved to be far more mundane. The tablets turned out to be long lists. These recorded taxes taken, tributes given and objects such as military equipment used in war. Some of these were those taken from foreign settlements during raids: an ivory footstool, a pair of bronze wheels, and women.

The Linear B tablets also provided clues about the hierarchy of the Mycenaean city-states. At the head of each state was the king or Wanax (or in Homer also Anax), who was surrounded by an elite warrior caste called the *heqetai*. Homer habitually call Agamemnon 'Wanax [or Anax] andron'; 'king of men'. At the bottom of the social ladder was a peasant class called the *doeroi*. The food produced by the doeroi was used to feed the king and his heqetai, as well as the priests and officials who made up the civilization's middle class.

The tablets show the tight stranglehold the Mycenaean elite held over its territories: labourers, peasants and slaves were used in agriculture and the manufacture of goods such as textiles and Mycenaean pottery. The profit from this trade was rigorously controlled.

BELOW: **A Mycenaean clay tablet written in Linear B script.**

There was a clear gulf between the common people of Mycenae and its royal warrior elite, a caste whose wealth and power reached its zenith around the fourteenth and thirteenth centuries BCE.

As we have seen from the excavations made by Heinrich Schliemann in the Mycenae citadel, vast riches were spent on royal graves. Huge amounts of gold, bronze and silver were lavished upon weaponry alone. The scenes of hunting and fighting shown on the daggers of these dead, not to mention the colourful frescos on the walls of the palaces, show the preoccupations of the aristocratic warrior class and the veneration of the royal cult.

Kings such as Agamemnon needed to keep his warriors happy with gifts, food and the generous hospitality of his court. His military needed to be armed, trained and kept up-to-date and battle-ready with weapons and chariots. However, remote

BELOW: A Mycenaean noblewoman depicted in a fresco dating from between 1,400 and 1,200 BCE.

citadels such as Mycenae, while having control over agriculture and industry on the plain of Argos below, did not have access to gold, silver or even the tin and copper used in the manufacture of bronze. This was arguably the most important metal of this 'Bronze Age', as effective swords could not easily be forged from silver or gold.

Overseas trade, of which there was much between the Mycenaeans and other Bronze Age kingdoms, could only bring in some of the required revenue needed to support a warrior city-state. Mycenaean pottery, in particular, has been found in locations from Egypt to Anatolia, including within the ruins of Troy itself. But to turn a culture into an empire required loot, and that could only be acquired in war.

Mycenae was never an empire in the traditional sense. Instead, it was a confederation of loosely aligned city-states that owed some sort of allegiance to its most powerful member – Mycenae. A king like Agamemnon would have been able to offer his fellow aristocratic city-states warfare and treasure. The greater the loot, the greater the kudos for the conqueror who provided for its capture. And this, for the aristocrats who spent their time hunting, fighting and winning fame and fortune, was highly desirable. So these are the goals of the heroic kings and the warriors who fought alongside them: for honour, glory, wealth and the creation of a great heroic legacy that would live on long after their demise.

However, the complexities of this legacy are clear in Homer's work. He immortalized Agamemnon and revealed his faults and flaws. The hero-king is also a blustering braggart. Here

ABOVE: **Bronze Mycenaean weapons, including swords and daggers, were excavated from Mycenae by Schliemann.**

RIGHT: This nineteenth century Pierre-Narcisse Guérin artwork shows Clytemnestra hesitating before the murder of her sleeping husband, Agamemnon.

lies the wonder of ancient poetry, for it casts its spell long after the facts of history have disappeared. Judged by his supposed achievements, Agamemnon could be considered a great warrior king: a sacker of cities with an army of Mycenaean Greeks at his command. However, the personality we see behind Homer's Agamemnon is of a vain and arrogant leader, doomed to die at the hands of his wife and her lover.

The Hittites

The Mycenaeans were not the only important power region in the Mediterranean and Near East in the late Bronze Age. The others were the Egyptians, the Assyrians, the Babylonians and the Hittites. Mentioned in the Old Testament, the Hittites were all but forgotten during the time of the classical Greeks; even today, they remain somewhat obscure. But this was a great empire that controlled a vast tract of land across Anatolia. Hatti, as the Hittites called their empire, was a superpower second only to

MYCENAE: MAJESTY AND MIGHT

THE CLASSICAL GREEKS WHO discovered the thick walls of the Mycenaean citadels thought they must have been built by the one-eyed giants known as the Cyclopes. We now know that the walls were constructed by the Mycenaean warrior kings and paid for with foreign trade and plunder. The city-state that boasted the grandest architecture was also its most powerful: Mycenae. Visitors to this lofty palace citadel climbed a steep, paved road through its main gateway, where the two lions of Mycenae's royal coat of arms were carved into the black limestone.

Beyond the gate to the right was a great circle of upright stones – the graves excavated by Heinrich Schliemann – and to the left, the palace and royal apartments. With their commanding view over the plain of Argos, these royal rooms were designed to impress: the columned throne room brightly painted with colourful frescos showed scenes from hunting expeditions and war. A round hearth filling the centre of the room would have been attended day and night. This was the setting for evening feasts, where musicians played lyres and bards recited epic poems about the great deeds of their king.

An aerial view of the citadel of Mycenae as it looks today.

Egypt. The Egyptians, however, were not the Hittites' only rivals; another was Mycenae.

The Hittites emerged in around 1800 BCE as city-states that leaned heavily on the old Mesopotamian kingdoms in their cultural, religious and economic development. The Hittite culture was largely feudal, with the king – the earthly representative of the storm god – at the top, and serfs, artisans, and slaves at the bottom. Many of these laboured in the mines across Anatolia, for Hatti was rich in metals, particular the silver and tin coveted by the Mycenaeans.

Almost everything we know about the Hittites comes from the thousands of cuneiform tablets found scattered across the floor of the king's royal palace in his capital of Hattusa. Excavated in 1906, the palace tablets showed the Hittites to be assiduous record-takers. Of great interest were those tablets written by the Hittite foreign office, which paint a graphic picture of the inner workings of the Hatti Empire and its diplomatic efforts with the other empires around it.

The tablets show that the superpowers of the age were something of a select club; only 'Great Kings' could become members. These 'Great Kings' were in frequent contact and their diplomats were kept busy delivering messages and gifts to strike trade deals, settle border disputes, lend military support and broker alliances through marriage. Letters between the kings employed the common diplomatic language of the day; using the correct terminology was an important part of these exchanges.

'Brother', 'Father' and 'Son' were some of the main forms of address, although 'Brother' was used only in a relationship between equals. The use of the term

BELOW: This Hittite cuneiform tablet is believed to be a legal document dating from around 1700 BCE.

ABOVE: The seal of the Hittite king Hattušili.

'Great King' was of particular importance – it was not a title that just any ruler could adopt. A letter from the Hittite king Hattušili to a younger and newly enthroned Assyrian king rebukes him for referring to himself as 'Great'.

'You brag that…you have become a Great King. But what is this about "brotherhood"? Are you and I born of the same mother? Far from it…so stop writing to me about brotherhood and Great Kingship for I have no wish for it.'

By comparison, Hattušili's correspondence with Egyptian Pharaoh Ramses II shows that perceived slights between 'Great Kings' could spiral into diplomatic incidents. Here, Ramses tries to calm and reassure Hattušili after the Hittite accuses him of addressing him as though he were a subject:

ABOVE: **A Corinthian-style helmet, dating from around 500 BCE.**

'I have just heard all the words that you have written to me my brother, saying: "Why did you, my brother, write to me as if I were a mere subject of yours?" I resent what you write to me, my brother. You have accomplished great things in all lands; you are indeed a Great King in the Hatti lands… Why should I write to you as though to a subject?'

If the Egyptians were sure the Hittite ruler was a 'Great King' what did they make of the Mycenaeans? Would Agamemnon be known as 'Great'? Homer would have said yes. The *Iliad* refers to Agamemnon as 'lord of all Argos and of the isles'.

The Hittites would have concurred. Among the cuneiform tablets found at Hattusa are correspondence to the 'King of Ahhiyawa', which also refer to him as a 'Great King'. Deciphering the phrase 'King Of Ahhiyawa' was a breakthrough moment. 'Ahhiyawa' referred to the 'Achaea land', domain of the Mycenaean Greeks. In the early twentieth century, this interpretation was contentious: only recently have scholars generally agreed that Ahhiyawa definitely refers to the Achaeans.

This is important, because it shows that to the Hittites, the Ahhiyawa were officially one of the great Bronze Age superpowers. They were also the Hittites' main western neighbour. And as the cuneiform tablets describe, the relationship between the two superpowers was a familiar story of tense mutual suspicion that somehow combined trade and diplomacy with border disputes and outbreaks of violence.

One of the earliest recorded outbreaks was in the mid-fifteenth century BCE, according to the cuneiform text. It says the Ahhiyawa ruler called Attarissiya sailed to the west coast of

Anatolia with the express purpose of fighting the Hittites. The battle featured thousands of infantry and more than 100 chariots. This was a large force by any Bronze Age standard, especially 200 years before the Trojan War is believed to have taken place.

The Western Front

The cuneiform tablets from Hattusa revealed the western Anatolia as a fractious region of the Hatti Empire. Hittite control in this area was often shaky, and the city-states often changed hands. Western Anatolia seems to have had something of a frontier mentality, where opportunists and adventurers often became embroiled in local power struggles and rebellions against the king in Hattusa.

One such man was Piyama-Radu, a Hittite noble who had fallen out of favour at the royal court and was now causing trouble in western Anatolia. The story helps establish the Mycenae as one of the superpowers of the Bronze Age and suggests that Wilusa, or Troy, was a pawn or proxy state in the

WHAT'S IN A NAME?

FOR MOST MODERN SCHOLARS, the cuneiform tablets found at Hattusa provide evidence that the Mycenaeans, or Ahhiyawa as the Hittites knew them, were actively involved in raiding, trading and invading in the Hatti Empire, especially along its western coast. Further investigation of the cuneiform tablets found many other Hittite words for Mycenaean names, thus bringing Mycenae, Hatti and Troy tantalizingly close together. The most compelling of these Hittite names and their probable translations are listed below:

HITTITE	MYCENAEAN GREEK
Millawanda	Miletus (an Anatolian city-state, sometimes controlled by the Ahhiyawa)
Wilusa	Wilios (Troy)
Alaksandu	Alexander (Homer's other name for Paris)
Tawagalawa	Eteocles (King of Thebes, according to Homer)
Attarissiya	Atreus (Father of Agamemnon and Melenaus, according to Homer)

shifting power struggle between Ahhiyawa (Mycenae) and the Hittites. The story of Troy, in brief, might be the story of one of the battles between the superpower Mycenae and a renegade king who had turned against his fellow Hittites, the other superpower of the day.

In the thirteenth century BCE, Piyama-Radu apparently launched a series of raids on the Hittite city-states dotted around western Anatolia and installed himself as overlord of Wilusa (Troy). Backing him was the Greek prince called Tawagalawa (Eteocles of Thebes), ruler of Millawanda (Miletus in Anatolia). This was of great concern to the Hittites, since Wilusa had previously shown loyalty to the Hittite crown.

> Featuring more than 6000 chariots, Kadesh is believed to have been the largest such battle in history.

A Hittite king known as Muwatalli II responded to the treacherous Piyama-Radu by marching an army to Millawanda. Muwatalli is best known for his part in the 1274 BCE Battle of Kadesh with the Egyptian Pharaoh Ramses II. Featuring more than 6000 chariots, Kadesh is believed to have been the largest such battle in history, but one that ended in a stalemate. Afterwards the matter was resolved with one of the first known international peace treaties in history. A clay copy of the treaty was found among the cuneiform tablets at Hattusa.

Meanwhile in Anatolia, Muwatalli and his army reached Wilusa only to find that the freebooting Piyama-Radu had fled, allegedly to Greece. He was also reported to have taken 7000 Hittite prisoners with him.

Because Muwatalli was chiefly concerned with tensions with Egypt on his eastern frontier, he made some allowances for the trouble in western Anatolia. Most notable was his acceptance that Millawanda could remain in Ahhiyawan hands, despite it originally being a vassal of Hatti. Muwatalli now dealt with the matter of Wilusa by installing a new vassal king, Alaksandu, and drawing up a treaty to cement their arrangement.

You, Alaksandu, benevolently protect My Majesty. And later protect my son and my grandson, to the first and second generation. And as I, My Majesty, protected you, Alaksandu, in good will because of the word of your father, and came to your aid, and killed your enemy for you, later in the future my sons and my grandsons will certainly protect your descendant for you, to the first and second generation. If some enemy arises for you, I will not abandon you, just as I have not now abandoned you, I will kill your enemy for you. But if your brother or someone of your family revolts against you, Alaksandu, or later someone revolts against your son or your grandsons, and they seek the kingship of the land of Wilusa, I, My Majesty, will absolutely not depose you, Alaksandu.' – THE ALAKSANDU TREATY

What is implicit in the Alaksandu Treaty was that the Hittites had previously come to the aid of the ruler of Wilusa against an attacking power. Exactly who the attacking power was is unfortunately unknown. However, another document, called

BELOW: **This relief from the temple of Abu Simbel shows Ramses II in his chariot at the 1274 Battle of Kadesh.**

the Tawagalawa Letter, shows that another conflict was fought between the Hittites and the Ahhiyawa, and that the rogue Piyama-Radu had once again been at the centre of the trouble. In the letter, Muwatalli II or his brother Hattušili III asks that the Ahhiyawa king, Tawagalawa, exercise some control over Piyama-Radu:

Now according to the rumour, during the time when Piyama-Radu leaves behind his wife and children and household in my Brother's land, your land is affording him protection. But he is continually raiding my land; but whenever I have prevented him in that, he comes back into your territory. Are you now, my Brother, favourably disposed to this conduct? [If not], now, my Brother, write to him at least this: 'Rise up, go forth into the land of Hatti, your lord has settled his account with you!... From my country you shall not conduct hostilities... The King of the Hatti and I – in that matter of Wilusa over which we were at enmity,

BELOW: **This treaty between the Egyptians and Hittites after the stalemate at Kadesh is one of the oldest peace treaties known to history.**

LEFT: **The seal of Hittite king Tudhaliya IV.**

he has converted me and we have made friends...a war would not be right for us.' – THE TAWAGALAWA LETTER

The document, written out in cuneiform on a clay tablet, is interesting for two reasons: one, it addresses Tawagalawa as an equal, showing that he too is regarded as a Great King; two, the letter describes a direct confrontation between the Hittites and the Ahhiyawa over the city-state of Wilusa.

A later piece of evidence linking the events of Wilusa with the Hittites is the Milawata Letter. This is from one of the last Hittite kings, Tudhaliya IV, and describes Tudhaliya reinstating a ruler called Walmu to the throne of Wilusa after he had been deposed by an unknown power.

Walmu, who is thought to be the son of Alaksandu, is to be used as a 'military vassal', the letter says. If this lineage is correct, then the Hittites have stayed true to their word in the Alaksandu Treaty to 'protect your descendants for you.'

Finally, there is one last mysterious document that indicates a change in fortunes for the Ahhiyawa. This was a peace treaty between Tudhaliya IV and the king of Amurru in Lebanon. The Hittite king is offering advice in the treaty to this 'Little King':

'If the King of Egypt is My Majesty's friend, he shall be your friend...the Kings who are equals in rank are the King of Egypt,

ABOVE: An engraving
showing King Tudhaliya
IV, which was discovered
at the Hittite Yazilikaya
rock sanctuary in Turkey.

the King of Babylonia, the King of Assyria and the King of Ahhiyawa.'

But 'King of Ahhiyawa' has been crossed out on the cuneiform tablet. Why? Does this mean the king had died, or that the Hittites no longer regard the King of Ahhiyawa as 'Great'? Tudhaliya IV was not the last king of Hatti, but his reign fell between 1237 and 1209 BCE – irresistibly close to the believed time of the Trojan War. Did a final war between the two superpowers forever end the possibility of diplomatic relations? Or did it irrecoverably diminish the status of the Ahhiyawa?

Superpower battles

Let's summarize these complicated events. During the early thirteenth century, a Hittite rebel called Piyama-Radu assumed control over Wilusa with backing from the Ahhiyawa. The Hittities then led a force to Wilusa and installed a vassal king called Alaksandu in Piyama-Radu's stead. Then, some decades later, Alaksandu's son Walmu was deposed and consequently restored by the Hittite king Tudhaliya IV.

So where does any of this get us with the Trojan War?

It is eminently likely that these events describe Mycenaean attacks on Troy during the reign of a king called Paris. We know that at least one large battle took place between the two superpowers of Hatti and Mycenae in the fifteenth century and that city-states such as Miletus on the western coast of Anatolia changed hands at least twice. So did another great battle take place around the time of Paris? Was this responsible for toppling his heir Walmu? What happened in the final scene at Troy VII, the city that, according to the archaeologists, fell before an attacking army? Who were the characters who played out this shocking drama, which combined bloodshed and devastation with the glory of battle?

The Hittite noble Piyama-Radu reminds us of the heroic warrior tradition of glory and honour and the search for a great legacy. The Mycenaeans, as we have seen, were certainly part of this epic tradition. Their world was dominated by nobles who spent their lives hunting, fighting and preparing for battle.

Our search in this chapter has been for the heroic heroes of Homer and their possible place in history. However, the most elusive character will always be Helen. It was for her, after all, that the thousand ships were launched.

There is no mention of Helen in the Hittite texts. However, there is a description of 7000 slaves taken from Hatti, many of whom were women. No warrior king would lead an expedition to recover a 'brother's' wife without the promise of loot at the end of it. Homer says so himself. It is to the role of loot and its relationship with women that we now turn.

BELOW: This stone relief of a Hittite war chariot dates from the eighth century BCE.

CHAPTER 3

The Role of Women

The seizure and enslavement of women is central to the story of the *Iliad*. The siege is fought over an abducted woman; women are promised as booty for hard-won battle. The women of the *Iliad* suffer the same fate as many caught up in Bronze Age warfare.

IN THE tenth year of the siege against Troy, Achilles finally snaps. Subordination and reason then give way to rage: *Sing, O goddess, the anger of Achilles son of Peleus, that brought countless ills upon the Achaeans. Many a brave soul did it send hurrying down to Hades, and many a hero did it yield a prey to dogs and vultures, for so were the counsels of Jove fulfilled from the day on which the son of Atreus, king of men, and great Achilles, first fell out with one another.*

— HOMER, *ILIAD*, BOOK I

OPPOSITE: **This 1626 panting by Guido Reni shows the abduction of Helen from Sparta by Paris.**

The falling out between Achilles and Agamemnon is over two women, both of them slaves. The first is Chryseis, the daughter of Chryses, a Trojan priest of Apollo. Chryses visits Agamemnon to offer a huge ransom for his daughter's return.

The soldiers of the Greek army support the priest's request, but Agamemnon does not. Instead, he denies Chryseis' release, telling her father that 'I will not free her. She shall grow old in my house at Argos far from her own home, busying herself with her loom and visiting my bed; so go, and do not provoke me...'

Dishonoring the Gods

Agamemnon's dishonourable behaviour, the antithesis of the heroic warrior king, causes the ire of Apollo, who hears Chryses' prayers from Mount Olympus. Striding down from the mountaintop, arrows rattling in his quiver, Apollo unleashes hell on the Greeks. Seating himself away from their ships, Apollo fires volleys of arrows at the men and beasts of the Greek camp. For nine days, Apollo continues his onslaught; the Greek funeral pyres are kept constantly alight with the bodies of the dead.

BELOW: **A Paul Rubens painting depicting the argument between Achilles and Agamemnon, after Apollo unleashes his anger upon the Greek camp.**

On the tenth day, Achilles does what Agamemnon cannot. He calls an assembly to find out why Apollo may have cursed the Greeks and how best to appease him. An augur called Calchas has the answer. But before he speaks, he seeks assurances against the wrath of Agamemnon. These given by Achilles, Calchas explains Agamemnon's refusal to release Chryseis to her father and the subsequent anger of Apollo. The plague the god has unleashed upon the Greeks will continue until the slave girl is released, Calchas tells the assembly. Agamemnon speaks; 'his heart black with rage, and his eyes flashed fire as he scowled on Calchas':

> For nine days, Apollo continues his onslaught; the Greek funeral pyres were kept constantly alight with the bodies of the dead.

Seer of evil, you never yet prophesied smooth things concerning me, but have ever loved to foretell that which was evil. You have brought me neither comfort nor performance; and now you come seeing among Danaans, and saying that Apollo has plagued us because I would not take a ransom for this girl, the daughter of Chryses. I have set my heart on keeping her in my own house, for I love her better even than my own wife Clytemnestra, whose peer she is alike in form and feature, in understanding and accomplishments. Still I will give her up if I must, for I would have the people live, not die; but you must find me a prize instead, or I alone among the Argives shall be without one. This is not well; for you behold, all of you, that my prize is to go elsewhere.

Once again, it is Achilles who takes the role of leader and tries to reason with Agamemnon. He asks that the king surrender Chryseis and accept payment in kind 'three and fourfold' if they ever achieve the sacking of Troy. Agamemnon spits back at Achilles that he will give up Chryseis: '…but I shall come to your tent and take your own prize Briseis, that you may learn how much stronger I am than you are, and that another may fear to set himself up as equal or comparable with me.'

'Golden-haired' Briseis is the woman captured by Achilles during the sacking of Lyrnessus, a previous conflict where the warrior fought alongside Agamemnon. Now Agamemnon sends

two heralds to take Achilles' prize and bed companion. This is how Agamemnon unleashes Achilles' rage and his destructive anger is the subject of the *Iliad*. The Greeks went to Troy over a queen, but the expedition nearly fails because of an argument over a slave woman.

The absence of Achilles from the fighting line brings disaster for Agamemnon. After a crippling series of defeats, the king's army is hemmed in on its beachfront encampment. Looming over them is Hector's army, his warriors' many fires punctuating the blackness of the plain. Among the Greeks, 'panic, companion of cold terror' is rife as Agamemnon stands before his men in tears. He has been deceived by Zeus; the only solution is to run away by ship to the 'beloved land of our fathers'.

The army stands stunned as Nestor suggests an emergency council in Agamemnon's tent. Here, he remonstrates with Agamemnon and asks him to invite Achilles back to the fray 'both with presents and fair speeches that may conciliate him'. This excites Agamemnon, as he is sure Achilles can be won

OPPOSITE: **This Roman fresco shows Achilles being forced to give up the slave girl, Briseis.**

BELOW: **In this 1940 painting of the Judgement of Paris, the Trojan prince chooses Aphrodite as the fairest goddess. Hera would never forgive this outrage.**

WOMEN OF THE *ILIAD*

HELEN AND BRISEIS ARE the pivotal female characters in the *Iliad*. It is Helen's abduction by Paris that leads to the Trojan War, and Briseis' abduction by Agamemnon that leads to Achilles' refusal to fight. Her release by Agamemnon is then connected to Achilles' return to battle and the death of Hector; the moment that turns the tide against the Trojans. Both women are captives in their subsequent struggles.

As a personality, Helen is a paradox. She is both a bedazzling seductress, a whore and a home-wrecker and also a figure of fragility and a victim of circumstance, the motive for the war of men. Helen is trapped: she knows she is blamed for the siege and hated by the Greeks and Trojans alike; for them she has brought ruin to men. The Greek dramatist Aeschylus later calls Helen '*Helenaus, Helenadros, Heleptolis*': 'ship-destroyer, man-destroyer, city-destroyer'.

Helen's fate lies with the gods, and it is with Aphrodite that she argues after the goddess rescues Paris from the duel with Menelaus. Helen rages at Aphrodite 'who supplied the lust that led to disaster', but backs off when the goddess threatens to destroy Helen's beauty. As Helen goes to Paris, we discover that she does not hate Menelaus and, while continuing to love Paris, she also misses her homeland of Sparta and the 'comradeship of women' her own age. She has no choice but to remain at Troy until the gods reveal her destiny. However, at the end of the conflict she follows Menelaus back to Sparta to resume her duties as queen.

Helen and Paris are sometimes seen as reckless, wanton lovers who are the antithesis of the devoted and honourable married couple, Hector and Andromache. Andromache, unlike Helen, displays all the virtues of a temperate wife: fidelity, chastity, obedience and self-sacrifice. However, both women share the same dilemma: their lives are not their own. Instead, they are bound to the actions of the men in their lives, which are further dictated by the gods. In this, both women are prisoners of the patriarchal civilizations of the Bronze Age.

Helen of Troy. Was this the face that launched 1000 ships?

back with gifts and women. In the Greek camp, women are treated as commodities. He rattles off a list of all he is willing to bestow upon Achilles:

I will make amends, and will give him great gifts by way of atonement. I will tell them in the presence of you all. I will give him seven tripods that have never yet been on the fire, and ten talents of gold. I will give him twenty iron cauldrons and twelve strong horses that have won races and carried off prizes. Rich, indeed, both in land and gold is he that has as many prizes as my horses have won me. I will give him seven excellent workwomen, Lesbians, whom I chose for myself when he took Lesbos, all of surpassing beauty. I will give him these, and with them her whom I took from him, the daughter of Briseus; and I swear a great oath that I never went up into her bed, nor have been with her after the manner of men and women. All these things will I give him now down, and if hereafter the gods vouchsafe me to sack the city of Priam, let him come when we Achaeans are dividing the spoil, and load his ship with gold and bronze to his liking; furthermore let him take twenty Trojan women, the loveliest after Helen herself.

– HOMER, *ILIAD*, BOOK IX

ABOVE: The gold 'mask of Agamemnon' found by Heinrich Schliemann when excavating Mycenae.

In the end, the women of Troy are captured during its fall and divided up among the conquering Greeks, along with the other

ABOVE: **Briseis is returned to Achilles by Nestor in this painting by Peter Paul Rubens.**

spoils or war. Achilles would not benefit from Agamemnon's promise of twenty Trojan women, 'the loveliest after Helen herself', for he was dead. The Greeks sacrificed Polyxena on the grave of Achilles to honour him; the house of Priam was extinguished with her passing.

The fate of the enslaved Trojan women would be to work out their remaining days as menials on the estates of the Mycenaean nobles – or as concubines in their beds. This is where the myth of the Trojan War combines uneasily with the archaeology discovered in Mycenae: there is no question that women were abducted in large numbers from their homes around the Aegean and forced to foreign shores as slaves.

The Pylos Tablets

Nestor, the king of Pylos in the Peloponnese, was an elder statesman during Homer's Trojan War. Too old for the frontline, Nestor was an experienced leader who could reason with Agamemnon when the Greeks seemed doomed. Nestor was one of the few Greeks to return from Troy unscathed, although, according to the archaeological evidence, the historical Pylos was actually destroyed during the thirteenth century BCE.

During his excavation of the Pylos citadel, archaeologist Carl Blegen famously found a cache of around a thousand Linear B tablets. The tablets contained lists of possessions, including those of female slaves taken from the Hittite shores of Anatolia.

Among the lists of the slaves were '21 women from Cnidus with their 12 girls and 10 boys'; 'Women of Miletus'; and 'Women from Troy'. The last line provided a thunderclap moment for the world of archaeology: here was evidence linking

BELOW: **Slaves are auctioned off in this artwork of a slave market at Delos in Greece. The buying and selling of slaves was an everyday occurrence throughout the ancient world.**

Mycenae with Troy and the taking of women as slaves. It brings into sharp focus Agamemnon's list of women as gifts of appeasement for Achilles.

The Linear B tablets show us that the Mycenaeans operated as predatory raiders across the length and breadth of the Aegean Sea. Their loot often consisted of women, usually separated from their slain men and carried off with their children. The only other way to procure slaves was from a market. One such market existed at Miletus in western Anatolia, a city-state that often changed hands between the Mycenaeans and Hittites.

The fragility of Bronze Age settlements meant that a large force was not needed to sack a small city and take captives; a few ships often did the job. The Sea Peoples, who brought down many Aegean civilizations in the twelfth century, were sometimes equipped with only around seven ships. However, to take a large city, a confederation of city-states was brought together. It is likely that on such occasions a powerful king such as Agamemnon would have led the group.

The Mycenaeans were certainly not the only raiders operating in the Aegean. Piyama-Radu was a high-profile Hittite raider happy to enslave his own people. He also had higher aspirations, which included proclaiming himself ruler of Wilusa (Troy). He almost certainly wished for a legacy

BELOW: **A Linear B tablet found at Pylos.**

PYLOS PEOPLE LISTS

MANY OF THE PEOPLE listed in the Pylos Linear B tablets came from territories around the eastern Aegean, including Miletus, Lemnos, Zephyrus, Chios and Aswija. Aswija is a name found at other Mycenaean sites and probably refers to Lydia, or Assuwa in Hittite, the place that gives its name to Asia. The tablets refer to 'lawiaai', or captives, who were taken from Anatolia in their hundreds: 750 women are mentioned, along with their children, 400 girls and 300 boys. This tallies with a record from the Hittite cuneiform tablets found at Hattusa. These report that the freebooting Hittite noble Piyama-Radu sailed away from Anatolian shores with 7000 prisoners. However, slaves were not only taken from Hatti. According to Homer, the Mycenaeans abducted women from their own waters, including from the islands of Lesbos, Tenedos and Skyros.

as a 'sacker of cities' – a coveted title, according to Homer – Agamemnon, Achilles, Odysseus and even the goddess Athena all used it as a badge of honour.

Piyama-Radu wanted a piece of what the Homeric heroes already had, a glorious reputation as a 'sacker of cities' and the wealth that came with it. The loot from raiding was immense: gold, silver, bronze, weapons, armour, horses and women. The 'city and its women' is often mentioned in the *Iliad*; Achilles tells Odysseus that he has sacked 23 cities with 'treasure and women' as his payment. Beautiful women are considered to be worth more, as Agamemnon divulges himself when he offers Achilles 'twenty Trojan women, the loveliest after Helen herself.'

With this, one of the prime motives of the heroic warrior kings of the Bronze Age is revealed: wealth and glory, with the finest prize – the most beautiful women – to go to the leaders of the raiding parties. Honour and wealth won for the kings the loyalty of warrior aristocrats. These warriors were an essential part of any city-state's military makeup. The larger the target, the larger the force needed.

Homer tells us a thousand ships were sent to retrieve the enslaved Helen from Troy. But is Helen herself just a metaphor for the great number of Trojan women who were there for the taking? What was to be the fate of these Anatolian women, defined as 'booty' in the Linear B tablets? Was their primary purpose as sex slaves in the bedchambers of the Mycenaean nobility, or were they needed as menials for forced labour? Perhaps most crucially, how great was the Mycenaean need for slaves? Would a foray abroad have been launched with this purpose in mind?

The Labour Market

For the most part, the hundreds of female slaves brought to the sandy shores of Pylos did manual work. This was assigned by the palace officials and at the top end included carding wool, spinning thread, weaving, sewing and embroidering cloth.

BELOW: **Ancient Greek slave girls as depicted in this magazine illustration.**

Low-level, physically taxing work included grinding flour, cleaning the palace, carrying water and preparing flax by the river bank. Others still were used as personal servants for the palace elite, although personal slaves were the exception.

The slave women did not receive wages but only a subsistence ration of figs and wheat of about 24 litres (5 gallons) per person per month. However, several Linear B tablets record a slave woman named Cassandra receiving up to 25 times more figs and wheat than her companions. One likely explanation for this is that Cassandra was a slave supervisor who may have had the task of doling out the rations. It is interesting to note that even within the ranks of Mycenaean slaves there was a strict hierarchy that mirrored that of the palace free women.

Pylos provides an excellent model of the palace citadels that made up Mycenaean Greece. Similar tablets were also found at the Cretan site of Knossos, another Mycenaean city-state that formerly belonged to the Minoans. Together, these tablets record information on more than 2000 free Mycenaean women. Of these, it is notable that the women with a religious office were entitled to lease land – a rarity for females at that time. It is particularly surprising when compared with the role of women during Homer's own time, or in later Classical Greece. Then, women had no rights to property and they were generally restricted to the home.

ABOVE: **This tablet is a bill of sale for a slave girl from ancient Macedonia.**

This is not to say that Mycenae was an egalitarian society: it was highly patriarchal and women did not have the same rights as men. However, Pylian priestesses enjoyed greater freedom. The Linear B tablets record 120 women with religious titles – Priestess, Keybearer, Servant of the God, Servant of the Priestess, or Servant of the Keybearer – as having access to materials such as bronze and textiles for use in their cult activities and personal use. In addition, they were able to exploit temple land for profit. One priestess was also recorded as having 14 female slaves.

The Tools of Trade

Slave labour was an important link between Mycenae, the Hittites and Troy. Both Mycenae and Hatti were local superpowers that grew their civilizations through warfare, trade

THE PALACE VIEW

OTHER THAN THE INFORMATION from the Linear B tablets, little is known about the noble women who inhabited the palaces. The women – shown in the fragments of frescos or inscriptions in jewellery – have fine dresses, are often bare-breasted, and wearing makeup and gold and bronze jewellery. The veneration of noble Mycenaean females would tally with the theory that the crown did not pass from father to son but from mother to daughter. We see this idea in Homer when it comes to Menelaus and Helen: Helen is the queen of Sparta and Menelaus king only through marriage. Some argue that this explains the strength of Menelaus' wrath over Helen's abduction; without her, perhaps his authority in Sparta was diminished.

More is known about the Hittite noble women, who were believed to wield considerable power at the royal court. The Hittite queen was also the empire's high priestess; she shared a seal with the king that enabled her to sign official documents. After the king died, the queen would rule in his stead, albeit alongside his heir. According to the Hattusa cuneiform tablets, this often caused problems with the new ruler's wife. One queen was Puduhepa, who corresponded directly with Egyptian Pharaoh Ramses II and even negotiated the details of his wedding to one of her daughters. It is telling of her position and power that Puduhepa rebukes Ramses for hurrying her over the arranged dowry – a

This tablet includes correspondence from Queen Puduhepa, wife of Hattusilis III.

sum she was struggling to raise after the Hattusa treasury house had burned down:

Does my brother [Ramses] possess nothing at all? Only if the son of the Sun-God, the son of the Storm-God, and the sea have nothing do you have nothing! Yet, my brother, you seek to enrich yourself at my expense. That is worthy neither of your reputation, nor your status.

– PUDUHEPA, QUEEN OF HATTI

and industry. The palaces of Pylos, Mycenae and Tiryns, for example, formed a kind of ring of fortresses around the plain of Argos where food was grown and other staples of life produced.

Slaves were a vital part of the economy, sustaining an ever-growing populace in imperial Mycenae. Mycenae's policy of expansion meant more mouths to feed: the birth rate rose during the 1300s and slaves, of course, needed to be fed too. This was also true of the Hittite Empire. In Hatti, most ordinary people were farmers, eking out a living while growing food for the cities. The cities were wholly dependent on them. The Hattusa cuneiform tablets record periods of great famine after the kings resettled whole agricultural communities following bouts of war. Without slaves working the farms, the empire might have starved to death.

These vast agricultural communities also produced surpluses for export. Wool, the main material used for textiles, was chief among these; Hatti and Mycenae both had a burgeoning wool trade. The Linear B tablets from Knossos reveal that more than

This is not to say Mycenae was an egalitarian society: it was highly patriarchal and women did not have the same rights as men.

BELOW: The ruins of Hattusa, a once great capital reduced to a windswept wasteland.

1000 slave women worked in the palace's textile industry. Here, wool had to be carded, spun and then woven into cloth for export. The tablets record the minutiae of this textile industry in long lists of numbers and calculations. They report that there were 100,000 sheep in Knossos alongside a small army of shepherds and shearers. Allocations of wool to the weavers, production targets and the amounts of finished cloth were similarly recorded.

Many female slaves were acquired from Anatolia because of their ability to work wool. Skilled slaves were a particularly precious commodity. In Troy, hundreds of wool spindles were found among the debris of Troy VI and VII, the cities believed to have existed at the time of the Trojan War. Troy produced its own wool and imported woollen products as well. Textiles made from Mycenaean wool seem to have had an exotic appeal in Hatti. Other luxury items from Mycenae were found at Troy, including decorated ostrich eggs, boxes made of ivory, and tripod bowls.

However, the most common Mycenaean product excavated at Troy was pottery. The clay pots manufactured in Mycenae, especially the so-called stirrup jars, are among the most ubiquitous artefacts found across Bronze Age settlements of the Aegean. Troy appears to have been one of Mycenae's biggest customers. In the rubble of Troy, Mycenaean pottery was found in great quantities dating

BELOW: **One of the thousands of cuneiform tablets discovered at Hattusa.**

from the sixteenth century BCE to the first half of the thirteenth. However, in around 1250 BCE the supply of pottery dries up. This would fit with the historical timeframe for the Trojan War.

Trade was not only conducted between Troy and Mycenae, but also the vast majority of cities across the Mediterranean. Numerous Bronze Age shipwrecks off the western and southern shores of Turkey have revealed that the Aegean in particular was a great network of shipping lanes criss-crossing between Mycenae and Hatti. One thirteenth-century ship wrecked off Turkey's Cape Gelidonya revealed a hoard of shovels, axes, picks and 100 copper ingots, each one weighing about 23kg (50lb).

Copper and tin from Anatolia and Cyprus were crucially important to Mycenae. Although their city-states closely controlled their own agricultural and industrial production, they were too small to be wholly self-sufficient. Raw goods, especially the tin and copper to make bronze weapons, had to be imported. We also know that some of these raw materials flowed in from Troy.

ABOVE: This imagining of a Greek slave market is based on a painting by W.S. Bagdatopoulus (1888–1965).

ABOVE: Detail from the
Warrior Vase found at
Mycenae by Heinrich
Schliemann.

A picture, therefore, can be painted of great Mycenaean merchant ships sailing from Troy heavy with tin and copper, bales of wool and horses reared nearby on the eastern plains of Anatolia. Perhaps the ships would contain slaves trained to work wool. Maybe the ship would otherwise sail via the slave market at Miletus to replenish Mycenae's labour force. After depositing their loads at port cities such as Tiryns, the Mycenaean merchants would once again sail east. Loaded up for the Trojan market would be stirrup jars containing wine, perfume and olive oil; woven cloth and other woollen textiles; and the bronze weaponry for which the Mycenaean warriors were famous. For the Mycenaeans, these were the tools that allowed them to keep control over their kingdoms and expand their influence through trade and warfare. The crucial element in both was slaves. Slaves were needed in agriculture and industry; warfare produced more slaves.

As we have seen in Homer, female slaves helped keep a kingdom's warrior aristocrats happy. For without the aristocrats, there was no fighting force and no political power base. To make sure they had enough slaves and treasure, the Mycenaean kings made regular armed raids on overseas settlements. Constant raiding and warfare was therefore a necessary aspect of almost all Bronze Age kingships, especially a superpower with expansive ambitions like Mycenaean Greece.

Sustaining the Splendour

Murder and the seizure of slaves are celebrated in Homer's poetry. To be a 'sacker of cities' was a title of honour and a source of kudos; it was earned with labour and worn with pride.

Splendour and affluence were all-important to those at the top of the Mycenaean hierarchy. The kings lived in ostentatiously decorated palaces with marble imported from all over Greece. Architects and interior designers probably travelled around Mycenae decking out royal palaces and homes in the most dazzling colours and designs. Living at the royal courts were entourages of warrior aristocrats, men who expected high levels of comfort and opulence at their leader's expense. Great wealth must have been needed to supply these warriors with treasure, slaves,

BELOW: This Mycenean stirrup jar was probably used to transport liquids and dates from around 1200 BCE.

armour, weaponry, and expensive gravesites. Then there were the needs of any city: food, water, basic infrastructure, building works. It must have given a king like Agamemnon endless headaches to run his city-state and to fund it as well.

Life expectancy for a female slave in Mycenae was short. This was a time well before modern medicine; many of the bones found in Mycenaean gravesites show death by infectious diseases such as osteomyelitis, a bone infection, and brucellosis, a highly contagious disease found in unpasteurized milk. Untreated, both diseases would have led to a painful death. Many of the victims in the gravesite were children under five. Life was harsh and short for Bronze Age slaves, so replacements were constantly required.

The Pylos tablets record the numbers of slaves – 21 Cnidian women, 10 boys, 12 girls – alongside the rather prouder descriptions of war equipment and other precious objects: an

SEX AND VIOLENCE

MOST WOMEN ABDUCTED AS slaves had to labour on the great estates of Mycenae. Other women were destined to be the sex slaves of their abductors. In Homer, King Nestor of Pylos fondly remembers Achilles' success as the sacker of cities and taker of women. The beneficiary of one of these raids, Nestor was awarded the beautiful Hecamede, who had divine looks and was destined to be his servant and bedmate.

There is a long list in Homer of places conquered and women captured: Iphis, a Scyrian woman, became Patroclus' bedmate; Diomede of Lesbos was destined for Achilles' bed; and seven other women from Lesbos would join Agamemnon's collection.

Homer does not mention rape in connection with these women, but it lies uneasily beneath the surface. There is a gangland mentality among Homer's Greeks in their murder of men and taking of women: Achilles slaughters Briseis' family and then takes her for his bed; the Greeks boast about snatching the women of Troy after its sacking; the women are playthings for the warriors' pleasure and an expected payment for their butchery. Nestor himself makes this clear: 'Let no man hurry to sail for home, not yet…Not until he has slept with the wife of some Trojan.'

The inherent sexual violence in this is never revealed in detail by Homer. However, he makes clear that for many Bronze Age women who were stolen from their native shores, rape was part of their fate.

ivory mirror, a figure-of-eight shield, a golden chair inlaid with silver, and a chariot decorated in crimson and ivory. Exotic objects made of precious metals were expected by the nobles of a Mycenae court.

ABOVE: **An illustration of the grave circle in the Mycenae citadel.**

Over the centuries, the Mycenaean kings developed a workable system for sustaining their lifestyles, but it was one that depended on the stability of the larger Bronze Age economy. However, from the thirteenth century BCE, when the Mycenaen civilization was at its peak, the Bronze Age world began to experience an economic downturn.

Part of this arose from the instability caused by raiding. The Mycenaeans were a part of this, but so were disaffected Hittite nobles such as Piyama-Radu. Around the periphery were more obscure groups; ship-borne pirates and chancers trying their luck. Some of these groups were later revealed as the mysterious Sea Peoples who helped bring about the Bronze Age collapse and plunged the civilized world into a dark age.

Raiding, however, was not the only cause of trouble: the city-states also faced overpopulation, crop failures and drought. At the same time, citadels and fortifications were being upgraded.

Something outside the city-state walls was worrying the Mycenaeans. It is likely that Mycenaean power in the eastern Aegean was also on the wane. Their city-state on the Anatolian west coast, Miletus, was reclaimed by the Hittites. Without control of the slave market of Miletus, the Mycenaeans may have had to look elsewhere for their slaves – perhaps to the north and to the city of Troy.

> Troy at this time was still the glittering jewel of western Anatolia, a bountiful prize for any 'sacker of cities'.

Troy at this time was still the glittering jewel of western Anatolia, a bountiful prize for any 'sacker of cities'. It was, of course, to experience disasters outside its own control, such as the earthquake that would do such tremendous damage to the city. With weakened walls and an infrastructure in disarray, would this Troy have been too much of a temptation for the Mycenaean Greeks, whose systems and cities had begun to decline? Would the sacking of Troy provide enough treasure and women to prop up imperial Mycenae for a few more decades? Would it bolster the Mycenaean labour force and placate the nobles' insatiable appetite for wealth? Was a grand foray to Troy borne out of greed – or necessity? Would the elopement of a Mycenaean queen such as Helen provide motive enough?

These are questions we will perhaps never answer, for the Linear B tablets of Mycenae are only lists of possessions such as slaves and objects. The cuneiform tablets of Hattusa are of treaties and laws, lists and letters. Nothing in these primary sources tells us of the sacking of Troy and the trauma inflicted on those who were there. Instead, these descriptions are left to us by the poets; their verses are a testament to the suffering of all women who have ever been caught up in war.

Victims of War
Homer shows the dreadful cost to women of war and siege. At Troy, Priam's daughter Cassandra is raped at the altar of

Athena by the Greek Ajax the Lesser and then taken as a slave by Agamemnon; she is later murdered by Agamemnon's wife Clytemnestra. Another of Priam's daughters, Polyxena, is forced onto Achilles' tomb and has her throat slit in sacrifice. Andromache is taken as a prize by the son of Achilles; her son by Hector, Astyanax, is dashed to death on the city walls. Priam's wife, Hecabe, is given to Odysseus as a prize but snarls at him so viciously that the gods turn her into a dog and she is able to escape.

BELOW: **Here, Priam's daughter Cassandra is attacked by Ajax the Lesser.**

ABOVE: **This Goethe
Tischbein painting shows
Odysseus reunited with
his wife Penelope after
his epic journey home
following the fall of Troy.**

Their devastation of Troy complete, the remaining Greek
warriors pack up for home. Many of them are fated to long,
turbulent homeward journeys and sometimes a bad end at
the hands of a woman. Agamemnon is murdered by his wife
Clytemnestra on the day of his homecoming. Diomedes returns
home to an unfaithful wife and a kingdom that no longer exists.
Odysseus, the architect of the Trojan Horse that undoes Troy,
has to see off the many suitors of Penelope, his wife of twenty
years. After slaughtering these suitors to a man, Odysseus
executes the female servants of the household who have been
their lovers. The bones of Ajax, Achilles and Patroclus remain
on the plains of Troy.

And what happened to Helen, as Troy fell to wanton
slaughter, rape and pillage? A similar fate seemed likely, as an
enraged Menelaus had sworn to murder her on sight. However,
her beauty once again dictated her destiny, for as her estranged
husband tore into her chamber with sword raised, Helen

unbared her breasts, and was forgiven. There were no further recriminations. Helen would return to Sparta and take up her role as queen, as before. One of her duties would have been to instruct those supervising the army of female slaves working in the estates' industries; women such as her, but without the royal blood or dazzling looks.

Helen and Menelaus are destined to become old together. In the *Odyssey*, Odysseus' nephew visits the aged couple in their Sparta palace. Helen invites him to 'sit here now in the palace and take your dinner and be entertained.' Helen then recounts the story of the Trojan War, including her attempts to fool the Greek heroes hiding in the horse by speaking to them in their wives' voices. 'Yes, my wife, all this that you said is fair and orderly,' Menelaus agrees tenderly.

Homer's last words on the Trojan War also come from the *Odyssey*. This time, Odysseus remembers the end of Troy. Again, the image is that of a widowed wife destined for slavery:

So *the famous singer sang his tale, but Odysseus melted, and from under his eyes the tears ran down, drenching his cheeks. As a woman weeps, lying over the body of her dear husband, who fell fighting for her city and people as he tried to beat off the pitiless day from city and children; she sees him dying and gasping for breath, and winding her body about him she cries high and shrill, while the men behind her, hitting her with their spear butts on the back and the shoulders, force her up and lead her away into slavery, to have hard work and sorrow, and her cheeks are wracked with pitiful weeping. Such were the pitiful tears Odysseus shed from under his brows.*

– HOMER, *ODYSSEY*, BOOK VIII

BELOW: **A stone relief showing Menelaus and his estranged bride, Helen.**

CHAPTER 4

The Savagery of the Siege

Violent death is everywhere in the story of Troy. Homer tells in horrifying detail how warriors die. Bronze Age warfare was indeed brutal, but death is never anonymous in the *Iliad*. Its victims are named and their lives invoked.

THE *ILIAD*, considered by many to be the first great book of the world, is foremost a book about war. Our understanding of the world must include understanding of war, because war is one of the engines of history. Homer's story shows the cruelty and brutality of war, but also their roots in rage and vengeance. Rage is what sends Achilles to sulk after his slave girl Briseis is taken by Agamemnon; it is what shakes him back to life as a warrior after the slaying of Patroclus.

However, it is not rage that motivates Achilles' comrade Patroclus; it is lust for glory and sorrow for the suffering Greeks that pulls him to the battlefield. After pleading with Achilles in tears, Patroclus is given permission to prepare for war. He dons his bronze greaves with clasps of silver, his richly inlaid cuirass, and hangs his 'silver-studded sword of bronze about his shoulders and then his mighty shield.' Wearing a helmet wrought

OPPOSITE: **This sixteenth century Noël Jallier painting depicts the fighting outside Troy.**

ABOVE: Achilles is here shown making a sacrifice to Zeus so he will protect Patroclus.

with 'a crest of horsehair that nodded menacingly above it' and carrying two spears, Patroclus is ready to join the fray. There, 'the screaming and the shouts of triumph rose up together of men killing and men killed and the ground ran with blood'. Homer describes Patroclus' entry into battle:

Patroclus went up to him [Thestor] and drove a spear into his right jaw; he thus hooked him by the teeth and the spear pulled him over the rim of his car, as one who sits at the end of some jutting rock and draws a strong fish out of the sea with a hook and a line…he then threw him down on his face and he died while falling. On this, as Erylaus was on to attack him, he struck him full on the head with a stone, and his brains were all battered inside his helmet, whereon he fell headlong to the ground and the pangs of death took hold upon him.

– HOMER, *ILIAD*, BOOK XVI

The classicist Bernard Knox notes that the simile of the hooked fish serves to emphasize the brutality of this killing. The death is seen from the outside, not as the man himself experiences it. The human has become a fish. Homer's description of Bronze Age warfare regularly has this unsentimental side:

Peneleos and Lycon now met in close fight, for they had missed each other with their spears. They had both thrown without effect, so now they drew their swords. Lycon struck the plumed crest of Peneleos' helmet but his sword broke at the hilt, while Peneleos smote Lycon on the neck under the ear. The blade sank so deep that the head was held on by nothing but the skin, and there was no more life left in him. Meriones gave chase to Acamas on foot and caught him up just as he was about to mount his chariot; he drove a spear through his right shoulder so that he fell headlong from the car, and his eyes were closed in darkness. Idomeneus speared Erymas in the mouth; the bronze point of the spear went clean through it beneath the brain, crashing in among the white bones and smashing them up. His

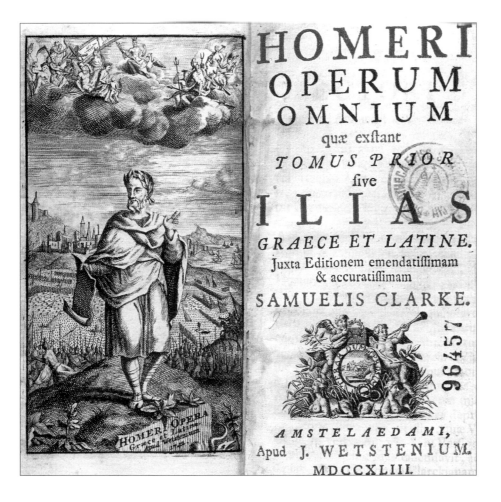

LEFT: A 1743 Latin edition of Homer's *Iliad*.

teeth were all of them knocked out and the blood came gushing in a stream from both his eyes; it also came gurgling up from his mouth and nostrils, and the darkness of death enfolded him round about. – HOMER, *ILIAD*, BOOK XVI

Many of the 170 battlefield encounters in the *Iliad* also give a vivid account of the life that has been so brutally ended: 'Hector only killed Periphetes of Mycenae; he was son of Copreus who was wont to take the orders of King Eurystheus to mighty Hercules, but the son was a far better man than the father in every way. He hit Pyraechmes who had led his Paeonian horsemen from the Amydon and the broad waters of the river Axius; the spear struck him on the right shoulder, and with a

BELOW: Hector tells his warriors to keep watch over the Greek beach encampment, in this ancient scroll.

groan he fell backwards in the dust.' The victim was a person with a background and a family and his death is regrettable. Death has a hideous human cost. Sometimes these biographical details give a special pathos to the death. In Book VI, for example, 'Diomedes killed Axylus son of Teuthranus, a rich man who lived in the strong city of Arisbe, and was beloved of all men; for he had a house by the roadside; but not one of his guests stood before him to save his life.'

Honour and Glory

While Homer shows that war is terrible, he also describes its glory, the rewards of honour and *aristeia*, or great moments of prowess in battle. *Aristeia* is what Patroclus yearns for when he

The hunger for glory and fame, or *kleos* in Greek, drove Mycenaean aristocrats such as Achilles to Troy.

enters the battlefield and it drives his wanton slaughter. War is what the warrior kings and heroes of the Mycenaean city-states left home for and battle would have been eagerly anticipated. This battlefield was the place where 'men win glory'.

The hunger for glory and fame, or *kleos* in Greek, drove Mycenaean aristocrats such as Achilles to Troy. Achilles' mother, the immortal nymph Thetis, had warned him of his fate. The choice was his to make: either live a long life in obscurity, or die young and gloriously on the fields of Troy. The latter would secure Achilles a legacy that would echo through time. However, he would die in Troy, struck down by the one weakness that had prevented him from invulnerability – his heel. Thetis had attempted to make Achilles immortal by dipping him into the River Styx as an infant. However, the part of his body that did

GRISLY ACCOUNTS

HOMER'S ACCOUNTS OF INDIVIDUAL deaths during the siege are swift, graphic and portrayed in shocking detail, sometimes to the point of physical implausibility.

Hector hit him on the jaw under the ear; the end of the spear drove out his teeth and cut his tongue in two pieces. After these he struck Chersidamas in the loins under his shield as he had just sprung down from his chariot; so he fell in the dust and clutched the earth in the hollow of his hand. The stone struck Cebriones, Hector's charioteer, a bastard son of Priam, as he held the reins in his hands. The stone hit him on the forehead and drove his brows into his head for the bone was smashed, and his eyes fell to the ground at his feet.

He hurled his spear, and Minerva guided it on to Pandarus's nose near the eye. It went crashing in among his white teeth; the bronze point cut through the root of his tongue, coming out under his chin, and his glistening armour rang rattling round him as he fell heavily to the ground. Meriones overtook him as he was flying, and struck him on the right buttock. The point of the spear went through the bone into the bladder, and death came upon him as he cried aloud and fell forward on his knees. Peirous, who had wounded him, sprang on him and thrust a spear into his belly, so that his bowels came gushing out upon the ground, and darkness veiled his eyes.
– HOMER, *ILIAD*, BOOK XVI

not touch the water was his heel, for this was where Thetis held him. Achilles would in the end be shot through his heel by an arrow fired by Paris. The slaying of the greatest hero of the war was carried out by its greatest coward.

Hector too was to win immortal fame at Troy, for this was the wish of Zeus. From his throne at Olympus, Zeus decreed glory for Hector 'and him alone among many men, for he had a short while to live.'

Homer shows us that fame could only be achieved by a warrior of great worth who performed an outstanding feat. This could include slaying another high-profile warrior, scaling fortifications to breach a city, or killing many opponents in quick succession. Most of the violence on the fields of Troy, therefore, would not bring fame for the warriors involved; this was available to only the bravest and best among them.

Hector was, in the end, faced with a quandary: to fight Achilles, retain his reputation and perhaps bring an early end to the siege; or to stay within Troy and play the long game, hoping his achievements on the battlefield would weaken the Greeks over time. It was an impossible position and, in a way, arguably the same as that which faced Achilles: to die in blaze of glory or live to anonymous old age.

ABOVE: **Thetis dips her son Achilles into the River Styx to make him immortal. The ankle where she held him, however, was not submerged.**

ABOVE: This Greek vase shows Agamemnon aboard his war chariot.

March into Battle

Homer shows that war is addictive:

'King Agamemnon,' said he [Nestor], 'Let the heralds summon the people to gather at their several ships; we will then go about among the host, that we may begin fighting at once.' Thus did he speak, and Agamemnon heeded his words...The chiefs about the son of Atreus chose their men and marshalled them, while Minerva went among them holding her priceless aegis that knows neither age nor death. From it there waved a hundred tassels of pure gold, all deftly woven, and each one of them worth a hundred oxen. With this she darted furiously everywhere among the hosts of the Achaeans, urging them forward, and putting courage into the heart of each, so that he might fight and do battle without ceasing. Thus war became sweeter in their eyes even than returning home in their ships. As when some great forest fire is raging upon a mountain top and its light is seen afar, even so as they marched the gleam of their armour flashed up into the firmament of heaven. – HOMER, *ILIAD*, BOOK XVI

This is the exhilarating battle march of an attacking army that a Greek reader would expect from a story about heroes.

Honour and heroism in battle are difficult to reconcile, however, especially during the confusion of a day-long melee.

Leading their men into battle in long columns were the kings and warrior aristocrats: they would include men such as Agamemnon and Achilles, at the top of the Greek army's hierarchy, and Paris and Hector at the Trojan's. Class was the great divider of a Bronze Age army; a warrior's rank could be instantly recognized by his armour and weaponry. Those at the top, such as Patroclus, would have been fully armed in bronze, including a plumed helmet, greaves, a shield, and a cuirass (a piece of armour protecting the torso).

The everyday soldier had far less equipment. They 'had no bronze helmets with plumes of horsehair, neither had they shields nor ashen spears, but they had come to Troy armed with bows,

BELOW: **A frieze showing a battle scene from the Trojan War from the Siphnian Treasury at Delphi, Greece.**

CHARIOTS

IT WAS TRADITION IN the Bronze Age that those at the top of the army's hierarchy rode into battle aboard a chariot. Chariots were the small tanks of the day; a line of charging chariots would have been a powerful disincentive for any frontline of standing infantry. Most Mycenaean chariots were light, made of wood and wicker, and usually towed by two horses. Driven either by a single warrior or with an archer riding shotgun, a chariot's great military advantage was speed and mobility.

Chariots were widely employed by all of the Mediterranean and Near East Bronze Age superpowers. The Battle of Kadesh between the Egyptians and the Hittites was fought mainly by chariot, with more than 6000 reportedly used. Hittite chariots were larger and heavier than those of the Mycenaeans and able to carry three passengers rather than two.

Despite the use of chariots in the Trojan War as reported by Homer, it is unlikely that large numbers of chariots took part in the fight for Troy. For the Mycenaeans, the transportation of chariots, not to mention horses, would have taken up valuable space aboard ships with limited capacity. The Trojans, while known to be great horsemen, would also have faced difficulties if they had relied on chariots. The terrain around Troy, sandy and unstable, did not lend itself to wheeled vehicles; the battles there would have been mainly fought by infantry.

This illustration shows chariots in action at the Battle of Kadesh, 1274 BCE.

LEFT: Mycenaean warriors
wearing their traditional
boar tusk helmets are
shown at the beach
below Troy.

and with slings of twisted wool.' The glinting armour of a warrior
like Patroclus would have been greatly prized and very rare.

Homer's battles were not like those of Classical Greece, where
tight phalanx formations took strict battle orders and worked as
a disciplined unit. Instead, Bronze Age warfare was messy and
disorganized. Often it centred on the individual and his personal
glory rather than the drilled effort of the united collective, which
came later in Greek military history.

The battles of the *Iliad* are fought at close quarters on an
open plain, like many pitched battles of the Bronze Age. First
missiles were fired, including stones from slings and arrows. We
are reminded of the power of the composite bow by Homer's
description of Pandarus, son of Lycaon, who fired a shot that
wounded Menelaus after his duel with Paris. This was the
moment that broke the truce between the Greek and Trojan lines.

Pandarus' bow was reportedly made from the horns of a wild
goat, and its many layers would have given it a special strength.
Composite bows could sustain a high degree of curvature while
the string was pulled back; although small and light, the bows
had a formidable range.

Once the archers and slingers had finished their business, the best warriors, or 'fore-fighters', as Homer called them, would move forward to the frontline. These were the elite, shock troops, well-armed and trained specifically for warfare at its most dangerous point. The frontline, however, would not have been static, but a fluid, ever-changing place that fed directly into the killing zone lying between the armies. Individual warriors moved constantly between the front and back lines. To engage in the fighting, warriors would step into the killing zone to hurl spears or engage an opponent in one-to-one combat with a sword in one hand and a shield in the other.

The bulk of the two armies were kept away from each other. No one was expected to stay on the frontline for a long time, nor were they supposed to skulk at the back. There was a sort of conveyor belt of warriors moving forwards as those injured or worn out retired to rest. Homer's warriors tended to stick together in small bands of familiars or kin as they moved forward to the frontline, although these often became splintered and separated during the inevitable chaos of military action.

Because of the coming and going of men at the front, the battles of the Bronze Age – and the *Iliad* – could last all day and have a number of break points. A breakthrough occurred when a great warrior was slain and a subsequent panic led to the breakdown of the frontline and a rapid retreat. This in turn would prompt a furious pursuit by the other side, urged on by their leaders' rallying calls. A typical day on the Trojan battlefield, therefore, might end only at nightfall, often with no discernible advantage to either side. In Homer the stalemate supposedly lasted for ten years.

Fight or Flight

The heroic code of warfare was complex. None of its heroes was above fear or even running away during moments of battle panic. This is not surprising when considering the conditions. Homer paints the field of battle between the Greeks and Trojans as a cauldron of sweat, dust and blood with thudding missiles, clashing arms and bellowing soldiers. It is incomparably loud:

'nor do the flames of a forest fire roar more fiercely when it is well alight upon the mountains, nor does the wind bellow with ruder music as it tears on through the tops when it is blowing its hardest, than the terrible shout which the Trojans and Achaeans raised as they sprang upon one another.'

The spectacle of the battlefield was truly dreadful. Zeus sent down a symbolic rainstorm of blood at the beginning of one day's battle; the rest was a chaos of hacking, lunging, stabbing and screaming. In the heat of the midday sun, limbs, viscera and bone would have littered the dusty plain as blood soaked the sand. Corpses would have lain heaped in various stages of sickly-smelling decay.

BELOW: A depiction of the Trojan War from an ancient illustrated Greek manuscript.

As we have seen, it was not expected for a warrior to fight on the frontline without taking a break. Nor was it expected that warriors would show an entirely fearless face to the world. Far from it: Homer's heroes were not 'fearless' warriors, but men who 'do not fear too much'.

Almost all succumbed to fear at one stage or other – even Achilles. Hector famously fled from Achilles and was chased three times around the walls of Troy before stopping to fight. Hector also retreated from Ajax and his heart pounded when he saw him; warriors throughout the *Iliad* are reported to tremble and change colour in the face of great opposition. It is for this Menelaus is told by his comrades to step away from a duel with Hector rather than 'to fight a man better than yourself'.

Homer recognizes that the greatest hero will have moments of fear or hesitation in battle, even if he is able to overcome it. In

BELOW: A frieze from Lycia, Turkey shows Greeks and Trojans fighting to the death.

BRONZE AGE WEAPONS

Although used for virtually all weapons of the day, bronze was not a particularly hard or reliable metal. Bronze swords had the reputation for breaking at the hilt or bending during battle. However, they were the mainstay of the Mycenaean and Trojan infantry alongside daggers and spears. Clubs, maces and single-bladed and crescent axes were also used.

SWORDS
The swords of the late Bronze Age were typically double-edged, around 140cm (55in) long, and made from a solid piece of bronze. They were used to slash at opponents. A shorter, single-edged dagger around 65cm (25in) long was used for stabbing at close-quarters. The longer and later 'Naue II' sword was around 85cm (33in) with a leaf-shaped blade; it came into use around 1200 BCE. The Hittites also favoured a sword with a

RIGHT: Bronze swords from Mycenaean Greece. Both date from between 1300 and 1100 BCE.

curved, or sickle-shaped blade, which was less prone to snapping; this may have made an appearance at Troy.

SPEARS
Long, two-handed ashwood spears, around 2–3m (6–10ft) in length with a 15cm (6in) bronze head, were the mainstay of Bronze Age infantry. The spears were used for throwing as a javelin and for thrusting against an opponent's facing frontline. Achilles' spear was said to be eleven cubits' long, which is around 5m (16ft).

A shorter, single-handed spear around 1.5m (5ft) long was adopted by the Mycenaeans in the late Bronze Age for combat at a closer range.

BOWS
Most Bronze Age armies were equipped with the composite bow made from laminated layers of wood, sinew and horn. Arrows, made of a wooden shaft and feathers for flight, were fitted with a V-shaped bronze tip that was difficult to remove without causing serious injury.

Book XI, for example, Odysseus stands against the Trojans who surround him: 'Ulysses [Odysseus] was now alone; not one of the Argives stood by him, for they were all panic-stricken. "Alas," said he to himself in his dismay, "what will become of me? It is ill if I turn and fly before these odds, but it will be worse if I am left alone and taken prisoner, for the son of Saturn has struck the rest of the Danaans with panic. But why talk to myself in this way? Well do I know that though cowards quit the field, a hero, whether he wound or be wounded, must stand firm and hold his own." While he was thus in two minds, the ranks of the Trojans advanced and hemmed him in, and bitterly did they come to rue it. As hounds and lusty youths set upon a wild boar that sallies from his lair whetting his white tusks – they attack him from every side and can hear the gnashing of his jaws, but for all his fierceness they still hold their ground – even so furiously did the Trojans attack Ulysses [Odysseus].'

Injury and Death

One of the striking aspects of the violence in the *Iliad* is the number of men who die instantaneously. Most exchanges involve only one, two, or a single round of blows – few battles reach a second round of blows. Instead, most stabs, slashes and swipes are either lethal strikes that cause instant death, or the assailant quickly retreats rather than try again.

It has been suggested that to add longer fight sequences to the *Iliad* would invite boredom for the audience, but it is more likely that Homer was simply exemplifying the skill and power of the attacking warrior and the swift consequences of his battle prowess.

As we have seen, the lethal blows inflicted in the *Iliad* have a destructive power that is sometimes hard to credit: blows to the head are delivered so strongly that eyeballs fall out; a jab to the stomach causes entrails to gush to the ground; a sword blow decapitates a man and leaves marrow spurting from his spinal cord; a man is beheaded with a spear.

The warrior hero of the *Iliad* is therefore portrayed as a man of great power who enters the fight when the odds are on his side and dispatches his enemies quickly and efficiently – the chivalric ideals of a longer duel are not always in evidence.

One of the striking aspects of the violence in the *Iliad* is the number of men who die instantaneously.

Another aspect of the violence that seems hard to reconcile with our modern knowledge of war is the absence of serious injuries. Most men are killed quickly: few are left maimed, moaning and writhing on the dusty plain, hoping for literature's first known field physicians, Machaon and Podalirius, to tend to them.

There are, however, some lasting injuries in the *Iliad*: Menelaus' wound caused by Pandarus' arrow is sufficiently worrying for Agamemnon to call over the doctor, Machaon. Menelaus is obviously in some distress, as he is lying down surrounded by his nobles. 'Machaon passed into the middle of the ring and at once drew the arrow from the belt, bending its barbs back through the force with which he pulled it out.'

Machaon then cleans away the blood and applies a salve, which perhaps contained honey, a natural antiseptic used widely in Bronze Age medicine, especially by the Egyptians. The Egyptians were expert surgeons, who used trepanning – drilling a hole in the skull – and also invented artificial body parts, such as a wooden toe. However, it is not known how many of these surgical techniques spread to Mycenae.

For battle wounds, it was understood that the weapons and debris piercing the body needed to be removed and the blood staunched with a bandage. Opium was widely used to treat pain, but there was no knowledge of wound treatment or infection. Any warrior unfortunate enough to be injured was at the mercy of their own immune system and, of course, the gods, who were believed to have the final say.

BELOW: The archer Pandarus, who would soon fall to Cebriones' spear.

ARMOUR

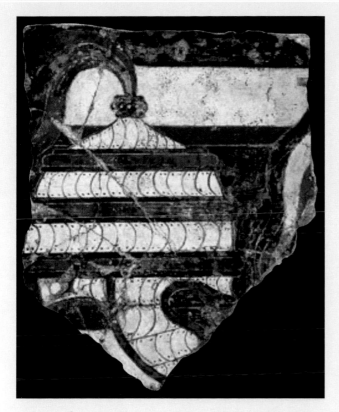

A fresco fragment from Akrotiri on Santorini, Greece, showing the Mycenaean boar tusk helmet.

THE BEST MYCENAEAN METAL armour belonged to warrior aristocrats. Those of the rank and file usually only had a kilt, greaves and breastplate made from thick linen and leather and a leather shield. Trojan armour would have followed the style of the Hittites.

HELMET

Mycenaean warriors are famously associated with the boar tusk helmet seen in frescos on the island of Santorini dating from the seventeenth century BCE. However, by the late Bronze Age, smaller, plumed helmets made of bronze or leather with cheek guards were more common. Hittite bronze helmets covered in scales with cheek guards were in use during the presumed time of the Trojan War. This was likely to have replaced older models with pointed tops.

BODY ARMOUR

A full suit of Mycenaean full-body armour known as a panoply dates from the sixteenth century BCE. Made of 15 bronze sheets held together by leather, the suit protected the wearer from his neck to his knees. Later in the Bronze Age, simpler and smaller bronze cuirasses made of plates with linen lining appear, sometimes worn with bronze shoulder guards.

SHIELD

Mycenaean wood, leather and bronze rectangular 'tower' shields that covered nearly the whole body, or 'figure of eight' shields are mentioned by Homer, but these were probably more widely used earlier in the Bronze Age. Shields from the late Bronze Age were made of bronze and mostly small and circular, sometimes with a half-circle shape cut out from their lower edge. The Hittites used a rectangular shield that covered the body from neck to thigh that was made from leather stretched over a wooden frame; a similar shield was probably used by the Trojans. Greaves made of bronze attached with leather straps protected a warrior's lower leg.

RIGHT: This suit of Mycenaean body armour was discovered in the village of Dendra, Greece. Made from overlapping bronze plates, the armour was found alongside a boar-tusk helmet.

The dead were left on the battlefield until the end of the day, when the corpses were collected. Observing the correct funeral rites was important for most known Bronze Age civilizations; the defilement of bodies after death was generally considered an atrocity.

One famous atrocity in the *Iliad* is the desecration of Hector's body by Achilles. Three times he drags Hector's body around Patroclus' funeral pyre and for nine days it lies in the dust behind Achilles' chariot. Apollo himself was disgusted: 'What good will it do him? What honour will he gain? Let that man beware, or great and glorious as he is, We mighty gods will wheel on him in anger – look, he outrages the senseless clay in all his fury.'

Achilles' treatment of Hector's body is a breach of the Bronze Age rules of war, but the age did not forbid mutilation of wounded soldiers or pride and even glee at the suffering inflicted on others.

ABOVE: **This seventh century BCE earthenware pot is decorated with a Mycenaean warrior.**

In one such instance, the Greek Peneleos cuts off Ilioneus' head and spears it through the eyeball 'as though it had been a poppy-head, and showed it to the Trojans, vaunting over them as he did so. "Trojans," he cried, "bid the father and mother of noble Ilioneus make moan for him in their house, for the wife also of Promachus son of Alegenor will never be gladdened by the coming of her dear husband when we Argives return with our ships from Troy." As he spoke fear fell upon them, and every man looked round about to see where he might fly for safety.'

Revenge is the main motive for defiling a corpse and in each case this is made explicit to the enemy. Agamemnon cuts off the head and arms of Hippolochus for offences against his men and then rolls the torso into the Trojan ranks 'like a log'. Menelaus does the same with the head of Imbrius, which he rolls to the feet of Hector 'like a ball'.

Other Greeks discuss their wish to capture an enemy and 'mutilate him', though sometimes this is justified as a means of demoralizing the enemy. Terror had a role in Bronze Age warfare, just as it does in its modern version.

Stripping the Spoils

In the *Iliad* there are many instances of warriors stripping armour and weaponry from the bodies of those they have slain. The most notable of these is when Hector takes the armour of Patroclus – which actually belongs to Achilles – after killing him.

Other examples similarly involved high-profile leaders. 'Agamemnon son of Atreus smote Isus in the chest above the nipple with his spear, while he struck Antiphus hard by the ear and threw him from his chariot. Forthwith he stripped their goodly armour from off them.' And 'as he [Diomedes] spoke he

BELOW: A 600 BCE Corinthian krater showing warriors fighting at the siege of Troy.

began stripping the spoils from the son of Paeon, but Alexandrus husband of lovely Helen aimed an arrow at him...Diomed had taken the cuirass from off the breast of Agastrophus, his heavy helmet also, and the shield from off his shoulders, when Paris drew his bow and let fly an arrow.'

Stripping a corpse was not only an accepted practice for the warriors of the *Iliad*, it was expected, even among its kings and leaders. Neither is it mentioned as dishonourable, or part of a ritual defilement of the dead; instead, stripping a warrior after killing him is a natural final act. The Greek Idomeneus boasts about this to Meriones, who comes looking for a spear before taking to the battlefield:

> Stripping a corpse was not only an accepted practice for the warriors of the *Iliad*, it was expected, even among its kings and leaders.

'Idomeneus,' Meriones answered, 'I come for a spear, if I can find one in my tent; I have broken the one I had, in throwing it at the shield of Deiphobus.' And Idomeneus captain of the Cretans answered, 'You will find one spear, or twenty if you so please, standing up against the end wall of my tent. I have taken them from Trojans whom I have killed, for I am not one to keep my enemy at arm's length; therefore I have spears, bossed shields, helmets, and burnished corselets.' – HOMER, *ILIAD*, BOOK XIII

The plundering of the dead therefore required risk-taking in battle, especially when it was a search for a trophy from a celebrated foe. However, as the example of Idomeneus shows, the more practical reason was to reuse the equipment in battle.

Homer describes in loving detail the warrior's arms, as shown in the earlier description of Patroclus donning his armour. Perhaps the most celebrated instance is his lengthy description in Book XVIII of the precious and elaborate shield made for Achilles by the fire god Hephaestus. Fine armour was prized both as a battlefield necessity and a source of prestige.

This would have been especially true for the nameless rank and file soldiers who fought with only rudimentary weapons and armour. Taking metal arms from a famous warrior would not

Odysseus and Diomedes here capture the hapless Dolon, who is promised Achilles' horses in exchange for information.

only have increased his chances of staying alive, it would have also been considered an expensive piece of loot, perhaps even an inheritance for his children. Nestor tells the story of King Lycurgus, who stripped his dispatched foe King Areithous of his armour and wore it himself in battle until he grew too old to fight. Then he handed it down to his retainer Ereuthalion, 'who in this same armour challenged the foremost men among us.'

Corpses were stripped during the fighting and when dusk fell and the battlefield was quiet. The dead were vulnerable to soldiers and profiteers, just as the *Iliad* constantly reminds us that they were prey 'to dogs and all the birds'.

Nestor reminds us of the practice of revisiting the battlefield to take from corpses; he warns his men against stopping to loot and therefore losing their impetus against the enemy: 'Nestor shouted to the Argives, saying, "My friends, Danaan warriors, servants of Mars, let no man lag that he may spoil the dead, and bring back much booty to the ships. Let us kill as many as we can; the bodies will lie upon the plain, and you can despoil them later at your leisure."'

It is no surprise then, that later in the *Iliad* the Greeks Odysseus and Diomedes, who are on a covert mission to spy on the Trojan camp, come across Dolon, a Trojan spy whom they mistake for a scavenger of the dead. Dolon cuts something of a tragic figure, a simple soul who has been picked out by Hector for his speed to spy on the Greek encampment on the beach. He is dressed in a wolf-skin, with a ferret-skin hat and a bow across his shoulder, and he asks Hector to swear a promise of payment: a bronze chariot and the finest two horses that belong to Achilles

himself. An attractive share, therefore, of the hoped-for war loot from the Greeks. However, Hector's 'oath was bootless', Homer tells us. As Dolon picks his way through the dead towards the Greek ships he is seen by Odysseus and Diomedes, who give chase and throw a spear over his shoulder to make him stop. Dolon immediately begins to weep and offers riches for his life: 'Take me alive; I will ransom myself; we have great store of gold, bronze, and wrought iron, and from this my father will satisfy you with a very large ransom.'

Odysseus assures Dolon that he will not be slain and asks him whether he is scavenging off the dead or has instead been

BRONZE AGE ATROCITIES

This relief shows the Egyptian pharaoh, Seti I, armed with weapons and ready for battle.

THE MYCENAEANS WERE NOT the only Bronze Age superpower to commit great atrocities against people in times of war. The Egyptians, Assyrians and Hittites all did so. The Egyptians are often considered to have had the most sophisticated ancient culture. However, according to hieroglyphs on the hypostyle wall in Egypt's Karnak, the Pharaoh Seti I 'rejoices to begin battle, he is delighted to enter into it, his heart is satisfied at seeing blood, he cuts off the heads of the rebellious-hearted, he loves an hour of battle more than a day of rejoicing. His majesty slays them at one time. He leaves not a limb among them, and he that escapes his band as a living captive is carried off to Egypt.'

Seti I was not the only pharaoh with a love of violence. After slaughtering 6000 enemies in Libya, Pharaoh Merneptah cut off their hands and penises to prove the number defeated.

sent by Hector. Dolon blabs freely about Hector's orders and the prize that awaits him at the end of it. Odysseus replies that it is unlikely any could handle Achilles' horses but the warrior himself and then asks where Hector's horses and armour lie. Once again, Dolon tells them everything: details about the Trojan camp and also of King Rhesus' fine horses and golden chariot; great prizes that pique the interest of Odysseus and Diomedes.

However, it is a trick, for the Greeks will not let Dolon live. Diomedes strikes him in the neck 'and cut through both sinews so that his head fell rolling in the dust while he was yet speaking.' Odysseus and Diomedes make their way through 'the fallen

The Assyrians had a fearsome reputation for violence. The late Bronze Age king Shalmaneser I boasted of conquering and looting more than 51 enemy cities, enslaving their people and blinding over 14,400 enemy prisoners in one eye. Battle scenes from Assyrian wall reliefs variously show scenes of torture such as impaling and mass beheadings outside city walls.

The Hittites, it has been claimed, were one of the early originators of germ warfare, which they carried by introducing infected sheep into enemy cities. They would do this simply by leaving the sheep outside the city walls to be claimed by the locals, who would later become infected through eating them. The infection was believed to be tularemia, a bacterial disease that can be passed from animals to humans and causes death through respiratory failure if not treated with antibiotics. So all was fair in Bronze Age warfare.

Shalmaneser I pours out the dust from Arinnu, all that remains of the fortress he razed.

armour and the blood' of the day's fighting towards Rhesus and his men, whom they slaughter in their sleep. Odysseus then jumps on one of Rhesus' horses while Diomedes considers whether to take the dead king's armour or, instead, his chariot. In the end, Athena herself tells Diomedes to leave and the two ride back to the Greek camp.

The incident is painted with savage strokes by Homer. For the Greeks, nearly any tactic for victory and loot is acceptable, even the slaughter of sleeping soldiers. Hector, by comparison, generally prefers the honourable rules of war according to the heroic code, including pitched battles and chivalrous duels between warriors of the same social standing. In the *Iliad*, the atrocities committed are largely those by the Greeks against the Trojans.

The Greeks thought the only thing more important than loot, women, or the promise of a large reward was victory. We are shown this in book VI of the *Iliad*, when the Greeks are trying to gain the upper hand and killing takes precedence over all else. Here, requests for mercy with the promise of a large ransom are denied, as this sequence between Menelaus and the Trojan Adrestus shows us:

Adrestus rolled out, and fell in the dust flat on his face by the wheel of his chariot; Menelaus came up to him spear in hand, but Adrestus caught him by the knees begging for his life. 'Take me alive,' he cried, 'son of Atreus, and you shall have a full ransom for me: my father is rich and has much treasure of gold, bronze, and wrought iron laid by in his house.' Thus did he plead, and Menelaus was for yielding and giving him to a squire to take to the ships of the Achaeans, but Agamemnon came running up to him and rebuked him. 'My good Menelaus,' said he, 'this is no time for giving quarter. Has, then, your house fared so well at the hands of the Trojans? Let us not spare a single one of them – not even the child unborn and in its mother's womb; let not a man of them be left alive, but let all in Ilius perish, unheeded and forgotten.' Thus did he speak, and his brother was persuaded by him, for his words were just. Menelaus, therefore, thrust Adrestus from him, whereon King Agamemnon struck him in the flank, and he fell: then the son of Atreus planted his foot upon his breast to draw his spear from the body.

— HOMER, *ILIAD*, BOOK VI

This is one of the rare occasions when the poet openly gives his own opinion. Agamemnon's brutality, Homer says, was 'just'. Homer assumes that Troy could not be taken without war, and war could not be effective without killing.

However, even amid the violence and brutality of Homer's Bronze Age there were ideals of right and wrong in warfare. War often involved massacre. At the same time, death was often tragic. Sometimes Homer even seems, aeons before the advent of World War I poet Wilfred Owen, to be describing 'the pity of war'.

The poet also recognizes that rage could sometimes make a great warrior a terrible force for evil. And no rage was more destructive that that of the Greeks' greatest warrior, Achilles.

CHAPTER 5

The Death of Patroclus

When Achilles learns of Patroclus' death, he wails inconsolably. He wishes he had never been born, declares he wants to die and throws himself over the dead body. Many believe that Achilles' grief is that of a lover, rather than a comrade in arms.

WERE ACHILLES and Patroclus gay? It is a question that has been greatly contested, particularly in modern times. Ancient Greece had a long tradition of male homosexuality and many city-states and militaries followed a system of pederasty – a sexual relationship between a boy and an adult man. Some argue that the ancients did not even question such a relationship; of course the two were gay. Why else was Achilles so devastated by the death of Patroclus? Others maintain that Achilles' grief is that of a close comrade, a deep bond of brotherhood that can only be created in war.

The *Iliad*, after all, is a poem about the heroes of war and life on the frontline. It tells us about the love between warriors who fight together and the unbearable loss of a close companion. For Achilles this was Patroclus, the Greek hero who had been slain by Hector. Hector had killed Patroclus believing him to be

OPPOSITE: The death of Patroclus, illustrated here, was the event that spurred Achilles into action and brought about the end of the war.

ABOVE: Here, Patroclus
attempts to scale the walls
of Troy. He is prevented in
this by the god Apollo.

OPPOSITE: Hector is
shown here finishing off
Patroclus. A tug of war
then takes place over
his corpse.

Achilles, as Patroclus had taken to the battlefield dressed in Achilles' armour in a ruse to rally the Greeks. None had known the truth until after his death. Achilles had allowed Patroclus to fight in his armour on condition that he return after beating the Trojans back from the Greek ships. However, overcome by hubris and 'pride and foolishness', Patroclus had battled on, pushing the Trojans back to their city and attacking them at the gates.

Here, Patroclus tried climbing the angled walls of the city three times, but he was not to immortalize himself as the warrior that infiltrated Troy. Instead, he was warned off by the guardian of Troy, Apollo himself: 'Draw back, noble Patroclus, it is not your lot to sack the city of the Trojan chieftains, nor yet will it be that of Achilles who is a far better man than you are.'

Apollo allows Patroclus one last kill, that of Hector's charioteer, before knocking the helmet from his head. He then makes his shield fall and undoes the fastenings of his cuirass. Dazed and vulnerable, Patroclus is speared through the stomach by Hector. Hector brags over the dying warrior:

'Patroclus,' said he, 'you deemed that you should sack our city, rob our Trojan women of their freedom, and carry them off in your ships to your own country. Fool; Hector and his fleet of horses were ever straining their utmost to defend them. I am foremost of all the Trojan warriors to stave the day of bondage from off them; as for you, vultures shall devour you here. Poor wretch, Achilles with all his bravery availed you nothing; and yet I ween when you left him he charged you straitly saying, "Come not back to the ships, knight Patroclus, till you have rent the

*bloodstained shirt of murderous Hector about his body." Thus
I ween did he charge you, and your fool's heart answered him
"yea" within you.'*
— HOMER, *ILIAD*, BOOK XVI

Afterwards a savage battle breaks out as the Trojans and
Greeks fight like hyenas over Patroclus' corpse. It is a terrible
tug-of-war in which the body is torn at and stretched as Hector
tries to drag Patroclus back to Troy. Once there, he means to
behead him and stick his head on a stake atop the city walls. He
would then feed Patroclus' headless corpse to the dogs of Troy.
But Hector will not have his prize. Menelaus strides forward
and stands over Patroclus' body to protect it; Hector has to be
satisfied with plundering the
armour.

The killing is a great
blow to the Greeks:
even Achilles' immortal
horses stand away from
the battlefield in shock.
Menelaus and Meriones are
able to lift Patroclus' body
above their heads and carry
him for a short distance.
Seeing this, the Trojans cry
out and fly at the warriors
like 'hounds attacking a
wounded boar'. Menelaus,
however, manages to scatter
the Trojans and the struggle
for Patroclus continues.

Meanwhile, Antilochus,
Achilles' lieutenant, brings
him the terrible news. As
Achilles listens, a 'dark
cloud of grief' falls upon
him. He grabs handfuls

of dust from the ground and smears it over his head and face. He flings himself down and tears at his hair as his female slaves scream aloud and beat their breasts in sorrow. Achilles' cry is heard by his mother, the sea nymph Thetis, who comes quickly to his side. Here, Achilles explains to Thetis what has happened:

'My dear comrade Patroclus has fallen – he whom I valued more than all others, and loved as dearly as my own life. I have lost him...I will not live nor go about among mankind unless Hector fall by my spear, and thus pay me for having slain Patroclus son of Menoetius... I would die here and now, in that I could not save my comrade. He has fallen far from home, and in his hour of need my hand was not there to help him. What is there for me?... Even so has Agamemnon angered me. And yet – so be it, for it is over; I will force my soul into subjection as I needs must; I will go; I will pursue Hector who has slain

BELOW: After the slaying of Patrolcus, Menelaus denies Hector his prize: he strides over to the body to protect it.

whom I loved so dearly, and will then abide my doom when it may please Jove and the other gods to send it... Till then I will win fame, and will bid Trojan and Dardanian women wring tears from their tender cheeks with both their hands in the grievousness of their great sorrow; thus shall they know that he who has held aloof so long will hold aloof no longer. Hold me not back, therefore, in the love you bear me, for you shall not move me.' – HOMER, *ILIAD*, BOOK XVIII

ABOVE: Here, Achilles is shown the dead body of Patroclus for the first time. His mother Thetis is quick to console him.

As Achilles laments to his mother, the battlefield struggle for Patroclus' body continues. After being alerted to this by the messenger goddess Iris, Achilles stands and lets out three great roars with a voice 'of a trumpet that sounds alarm'. Hearing Achilles, the Trojans retreat in terror and the Greeks finally retrieve Patroclus' body. This is the great turning point in the war. Achilles will return to the fight and with him brings the grief and rage that will bring ruin upon the city of Troy.

ABOVE: Thetis, whose image is reflected in the shield, carefully examines the golden armour that Hephaestus has made for Achilles.

Rage, anger, fury. These are the words Westerners use to translate *menis*, the Greek word that opens Homer's poem. *Menis* is thereafter the story's leading motif. It leads Achilles into his falling-out with Agamemnon over Briseis and then, when combined with his grief over Patroclus' slaying, it consumes him. Achilles' *menis* is cold and dark; while it is upon him, he will show no mercy to any man.

The Merciless Achilles

Once equipped with the new arms brought by Thetis, Achilles is ready for war. The armour is so bright and dazzling that the other Greeks have to look away. Achilles, however, becomes more caught up in his rage the longer he looks at it.

Then he gathers his men around him and makes a speech before Agamemnon and an assembly. Now the action has come full circle to where it began in Book I. But this is the beginning of the end of the Trojan War. Achilles rouses the Greeks with a speech he says will 'put away his anger' so he can join battle with the Trojans once more. Except his anger is in no way 'put away': it has simply been refocused on the destruction of Hector and the city of Troy. Thus begins Achilles' angry butchery on the battlefield: 'So furiously did Achilles rage, wielding his spear as though he were a god, and giving chase to those whom he would slay, till the dark earth ran with blood.'

Book XX of the *Iliad* is a long catalogue of slaughter: Achilles strikes Antenor in the head, his spear penetrating the helmet and shedding his brain on all sides; Achilles strikes Hippodamas in

THE ARMOUR OF ACHILLES

THE ARMOUR THAT ACHILLES lent to Patroclus was said to make any man who wore it invincible. This is why Apollo struck it away from the warrior's body before he was slaughtered. The armour was an intrinsic part of Achilles the warrior – it is what defined him on the battlefield and led to the slaying of Patroclus. Without it, Achilles cannot fight. This is why he appeals to his mother Thetis, who in turn makes a tearful plea to Hephaestus. Will Hephaestus, the god of blacksmiths, craftsmen and metallurgy, make Achilles a magic suit of armour that will protect him?

Hephaestus tenderly tells Thetis that he wishes he could hide Achilles 'from death's sight when his hour is come', but knowing this cannot be done, promises 'armour that shall amaze the eyes of all who behold it.' Hephaestus immediately turns twenty bellows towards the fire, onto which he throws copper, tin, silver and gold. With hammer in one hand and tongs in the other, Hephaestus begins work on Achilles' shield. The description of the shield is lengthy and much celebrated. The shield, made up of five overlapping metal folds, is the most elaborate and precious ever made. It features contrasting scenes of a peaceful and a war-torn country.

These scenes include the sky, sea, sun and other celestial bodies; two cities, one featuring a siege; a field being ploughed; a harvest; grapes being picked in a vineyard; cattle being attacked by lions; a sheep farm; people dancing; and the great stream of Ocean, the personification of the sea. Once complete, Hephaestus moves on to the other pieces of armour:

When he had fashioned the shield so great and strong, he made a breastplate also that shone brighter than fire. He made a helmet, close fitting to the brow, and richly worked, with a golden plume overhanging it; and he made greaves also of beaten tin. – HOMER, *ILIAD*, BOOK XVIII

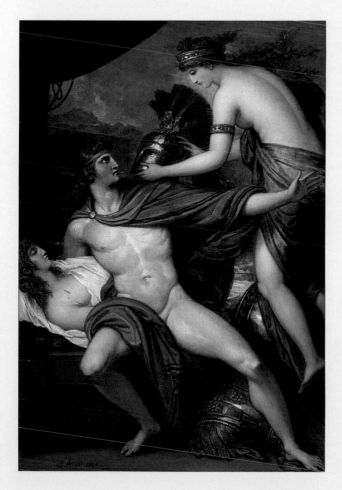

LEFT: Thetis presents Achilles with the armour made for him by Hephaestus.

the midriff, causing him to bellow like a butchered bull; Achilles spears Polydorus, son of Priam, in the back, causing his entrails to spill out from his navel; Achilles spears Mulius through one ear and out the other; Achilles severs the tendons of Deucalion's forearms and then cuts off his head so 'the marrow came oozing out of his backbone as he lay.'

Achilles kills 23 Trojans in a row, until his chariot axle is 'bespattered with clots of blood' and his hands 'bedrabbled with gore'. He then splits their army and chases one half down to the river, where they are trapped. Here in the river waters he continues killing Trojans like fish in a barrel, only pausing to take a dozen men alive as a sacrifice for the pyre of Patroclus. Here Achilles 'drew them out like dazed fawns, bound their hands behind them with the girdles of their own shirts, and gave them over to his men to take back to the ships. Then he sprang into the river, thirsting for still further blood.'

BELOW: Here, Agamemnon tells Achilles of his plan to sacrifice his daughter Iphianassa as an offering before the Greek fleet sets sail for Troy.

This is when Achilles is reunited with Lycaon, son of Priam, a man he once spared and held for ransom. Now caught again, Lycaon pleads for a similar mercy:

'Achilles, have mercy upon me and spare me, for I am your suppliant. It was in your tents that I first broke bread on the day when you took me prisoner in the vineyard; after which you sold away to Lemnos far from my father and my friends, and I brought you the price of a hundred oxen. I have paid three times as much to gain my freedom... Surely father Jove must hate me, that he has given me over to you a second time...I say, and lay my saying to your heart, spare me, for I am not of the same womb as Hector who slew your brave and noble comrade.' With such words did the princely son of Priam beseech Achilles; but Achilles answered him sternly. 'Idiot,' said he, 'talk not to me of ransom. Until Patroclus fell I preferred to give the Trojans quarter, and sold beyond the sea many of those whom I had

ABOVE: In this metal panel, Achilles is depicted aboard his chariot, his famous shield prominent.

taken alive; but now not a man shall live of those whom heaven delivers into my hands before the city of Ilius – and of all Trojans it shall fare hardest with the sons of Priam. Therefore, my friend, you too shall die. Why should you whine in this way? Patroclus fell, and he was a better man than you are. I too – see you not how I am great and goodly? I am son to a noble father, and have a goddess for my mother, but the hands of doom and death overshadow me all as surely. The day will come, either at dawn or dark, or at the noontide, when one shall take my life also in battle, either with his spear, or with an arrow sped from his bow.' Thus did he speak, and Lycaon's heart sank within him. He loosed his hold of the spear, and held out both hands before him; but Achilles drew his keen blade, and struck him by the collar-bone on his neck; he plunged his two-edged sword into him to the very hilt, whereon he lay at full length on the ground, with the dark blood welling from him till the earth was soaked. Then Achilles caught him by the foot and flung him into the river to go down stream, vaunting over him the while, and saying, 'Lie there among the fishes, who will lick the blood from your wound and gloat over it; your mother shall not lay you on any bier to mourn you, but the eddies of Scamander shall bear you into the broad bosom of the sea.'

    – HOMER, *ILIAD*, BOOK XXI

'He plunged his two-edged sword into him to the very hilt, whereon he lay at full length on the ground, with the dark blood welling from him till the earth was soaked.'

Achilles and Patroclus

The slaying of Lycaon is a telling moment that illustrates how soldiers can turn into heartless butchers through grief and rage. Lycaon is not the only warrior Achilles has spared in the past, as he says himself: 'Until Patroclus fell I preferred to give the Trojans quarter.' But now Achilles has abandoned chivalry and will not rest until Hector is slain.

    There is no question of the cause of Achilles' combat madness: it is his beloved Patroclus. So who was Patroclus to Achilles and

OPPOSITE: Showing there is no mercy after the death of Patroclus, Achilles here slays Lycaon.

COMRADESHIP IN COMBAT

THE *ILIAD* HAS MANY examples of comradeship in combat. Warriors from both the Greek and Trojan camps show their obligation to protect their fellow soldiers, to come to their aid when they are outnumbered, and help them from the battle when they are injured. They also avenge their comrades when they have fallen. As we have seen in the battle for Patroclus' corpse, the bodies of the dead need protecting too. The Trojan Acamas, for example, seeing that Promachus is trying to drag his dead brother Archelochus' body away, spears the Greek and stands over the body. He then taunts the Greeks: 'Argive archers, braggarts that you are, toil and suffering shall not be for us only... See how Promachus now sleeps, vanquished by my spear; payment for my brother's blood has not long delayed; a man may well be thankful if he leaves a kinsman in his house behind him to avenge his fall.'

There is also an understanding that each man's efforts in battle contribute to protecting the army as a whole. Hector shows he is not only the protector of the city of Troy but also his comrades. Even when he knows all is lost, Hector 'knew that the fortunes of the day had changed, but still stood his ground and tried to protect his comrades.'

To stand and protect his comrades on the battlefield is the role taken up by a guilt-stricken Achilles after Patroclus has fallen:

'I have brought no saving neither to Patroclus nor to my other comrades of whom so many have been slain by mighty Hector; I stay here by my ships a bootless burden upon the earth, I, who in fight have no peer among the Achaeans, though in council there are better than I.'

Now, in his grief, Achilles sets out to put this right.

what was their relationship? Were they simply close comrades in arms? Or was Achilles' grief and rage for his murdered lover?

Several passages in the *Iliad* point to a stronger bond between Achilles and Patroclus than just that of close battlefield comrades. A telling moment takes place during conversation between Achilles and his mother Thetis. Here, Achilles bares his soul to his mother, explaining that Patroclus, 'whom I valued more than all others', has been killed. When she brings him his new armour she finds 'her son fallen about the body of Patroclus and weeping bitterly'. This is a telling line because it is found elsewhere in Homer as the act of a woman grieving for a man. We see it later with the slave girl Briseis, who 'when she saw the mangled body of Patroclus, flung herself upon it and cried aloud'.

Later Thetis asks Achilles: 'My child, will you forever feed on your own heart in grief and pain and take no thought of sleep or sustenance? It would be comforting to make love with a woman.' Thetis' explicit advice to Achilles to sleep with a woman may be evidence that he was previously having sex with a man. However, there seems no criticism implied, but perhaps a reminder that Achilles should grow up and marry.

Part of the pederasty model, in fact, is the assumption that homosexuality is a passing phase that should end at a certain age with marriage and family life. Some scholars believe pederasty in ancient Greece came into formal practice during the Archaic period, and possibly originated in Crete. By the fifth century it was an accepted custom in many Greek city-states. Pederasty focused on a sexual relationship between an older man, an *erastes* (lover), and a younger man, the *eromenos* (beloved). It was the job of the erastes, who was usually a bachelor over the age of 18, to court his chosen eromenos, who was normally aged between 12 and 18. If successful in the courtship, the erastes would consummate the relationship through sodomy.

This was considered a way of introducing the eromenos to adulthood, an initiation into a

In classical Athens, pederasty was considered not only acceptable but at times an important aspect of a young man's social education.

male's coming of age. As the eromenos became a man himself, at around 18 to 20, he would stop being a passive sexual partner. Instead, he would seek out an eromenos of his own and take the place of the erastes in the subsequent relationship. By the age of 30, a man would give up the practice of homosexuality altogether and instead pursue marriage with a woman.

In Crete, the relationship between the erastes and eromenos involved a form of ritual abduction, during which the couple would ride into the countryside to hunt, feast and live in the wilderness for a couple of months. During this time, the erastes would teach the eromenos about the ways of men. Afterwards, the eromenos would be awarded with his military clothes and other gifts and was formally pronounced a man.

In classical Athens, pederasty was considered not only acceptable but at times an important aspect of a young man's social education. However, for this to be valid, the erastes'

BELOW: **This Attic krater shows the warriors at Troy in battle.**

intentions of the eromenos had to be borne from a 'heavenly' rather than a 'common' love. An erastes was expected to choose only one eromenos at a time who was at least pubescent or older and therefore considered to be at the age of reason. The erastes had to show his honourable intentions by courting his eromenos seriously and with determination. A dishonourable erastes would court several boys at once and was more interested in the physical aspect of the relationship and not their age.

If these were the models for the honourable and dishonourable erastes, what was the etiquette for an honourable eromenos? First of all, it was the job of the eromenos to resist the courtship. He would show himself stubborn and difficult to overcome, and when finally submitting to the sexual act would show no enjoyment. By following these rules, the eromenos could discriminate when choosing his erastes and therefore pick someone of high social standing. This would help the eromenos receive both social and material help, such as important contacts in the world of men and expensive gifts. It was, however, forbidden for money to change hands, for this would place the eromenos in the domain of a *pornos*, or prostitute.

Male prostitution was an acceptable part of ancient Greek life, especially in Athens, but free men who prostituted themselves were considered a risk to civic life and banned from any official duty. It was thought that if a man was capable of selling his body for pleasure, he was also capable of selling out his community for the right price.

ABOVE: **This bronze Corinthian helmet is from Greece's classical period.**

ABOVE: **Plutarch was a classical writer who believed homosexuality was a great boon to the warriors who fought together in war.**

Another forbidden aspect of pederasty in Athens was for a man over the age of 30 to put himself into the role of the eromenos. This was considered deviant, and men who enjoyed being sodomized were reviled as effeminate and could be deprived of citizenship if caught.

This model of pederasty, therefore, would not allow for homosexuality in the army. Soldiers were usually over the age of 20 and therefore too old to be an eromenos and would have to seek eligible erasti outside the military ranks.

However, this model was limited to classical Athens. There is solid evidence to show the practice of institutionalized homosexuality in the military of certain Greek city-states in the Archaic and Classical periods. The same practices among the warriors of Mycenae are more obscure, but the attitudes common in later Greece can perhaps shape our ideas about its more distant past.

Homosexuality within the military was widely acknowledged by Classical writers such as Plutarch. The Greek philosopher Xenophon wrote that some Spartans disliked the idea of a military unit made up of lovers, because this meant the fighting force was made up of those who found each other attractive, as opposed to those chosen for their fighting prowess. Xenophon wrote with disdain about military lovers from city-states whose relationships were based only on the physical without even time for conversation. However, Xenophon also reported the existence of homosexual coupling within the ranks of the Spartan army.

Xenophon's abhorrence of homosexual lust based on physical beauty was apparently shared by Lycurgus, the semi-legendary Sparta lawmaker who instilled the virtues of equality, military fitness and austerity in Spartan citizens. The Lycurgan system, in which Spartan boys were separated from women and reared on warfare, gave the Spartan military its formidable fighting edge.

According to Plutarch, when Spartan boys began their training at age 12 they would court the interest of both young adult men and older men too. This indicates that there was no upper limit on the age of a male erastes in Spartan pederasty – Plutarch mentions one who was 25 years old.

MILITARY MERITS

THE GREEK WRITER PLUTARCH has a lot to say about the beneficial role of homosexuality among the warrior elite of Classical Thebes – called the Sacred Band. The Sacred Band was a crack troupe of 150 pairs of male lovers renowned for their valour in battle. Plutarch's comments are telling, as the Sacred Band contrasts with the pederasty model forbidding homosexual relations between males of the same age. This is what he says:

The sacred band, we are told, was first formed by Gorgidas, of three hundred chosen men, to whom the city furnished exercise and maintenance, and who encamped in the Cadmeia; for which reason, too, they were called the city band; for citadels in those days were properly called cities. But some say that this band was composed of lovers [erastes] and beloved [eromenoi]. And a pleasantry of Pammenes is cited, in which he said that

Homer's Nestor was no tactician when he urged the Greeks to form in companies by clans and tribes, since he should have stationed lover by beloved. For tribesmen and clansmen make little account of tribesmen and clansmen in times of danger; whereas a band that is held together by the friendship between lovers is indissoluble and not to be broken, since the lovers are ashamed to play the coward before their beloved, and the beloved before their lovers, and both stand firm in danger to protect each other. Nor is this a wonder since men have more regard for their lovers even when absent than for others who are present, as was true of him who, when his enemy was about to slay him where he lay, earnestly besought him to run his sword through his breast, 'in order,' as he said, 'that my beloved may not have to blush at sight of my body with a wound in the back.' – PLUTARCH, *PELOPIDAS*

An example given by Xenophon reinforces the sense that there was no age limit for a Spartan erastes. He writes that when all was lost during one particular battle the eromenos of the Spartan leader Anaxibius stayed with him until the end, simply out of devotion. Couples were also reported to make a sacrifice to Eros before battle, as it was hoped the god of love would ensure their safety.

The loyalty and devotion formed between two lovers was only one way in which Spartans believed homosexuality to be helpful in battle. Another was that semen ejaculated during sex was believed to transmit the fighting power of the erastes to his eromenos. The similar insemination of Spartan boys in the gymnasium, where they were trained for war, was also believed to pass on the power and strength of the adult erastes.

Semen was highly valued in Spartan society and to waste it was considered a martial crime. It was understood that semen led to the making of children and was therefore a vital part of creating new soldiers for the army. If a Spartan man was able to produce three children he was exempt from serving in the military; his semen had done its work. By comparison, those Spartan men who could not produce children were considered ritually humiliated.

Plato describes the gymnasium as a site for the preparation of men for war but also for homoerotic behaviour. In Plato's *Euthydemus*, the boy Clinias attracts the attention of several erasti, including Ctesippus. Plato later said that the gymnasium's intention to promote valour among its boys through their close association was 'corrupting the pleasures of love'. Plato condemned homosexuality in his *Laws* and recommended that those guilty of it should be deprived of their civil rights.

Paradoxically, in Plato's *Symposium*, the character Phaedrus praises pederasty. This is notable, because it underlines the supposed acceptability of homosexuality until a certain age. Again we are reminded of Thetis' remarks to Achilles about making 'love with a woman' after Patroclus is slain. Is she indeed telling him that the expected homosexuality of his youth was no longer considered respectable at his age?

OPPOSITE: Here, Spartan warriors are shown defending the pass of Thermopylae, the great battle against the Persians in 480 BCE.

ABOVE: Spartan youths are shown here training at a Greek gymnasium.

There can be little argument that the bond of homosexuality within the military was considered a boost to its prowess. If Patroclus was indeed Achilles' lover, his death created a superhuman warrior in Achilles. Plato, oddly, agrees and theorizes about the invincibility of a fighting force made up only of homosexual couples:

So that if we could somewise contrive to have a city or an army composed of lovers and their favourites, they could not be better citizens of their country than by thus refraining from all that is base in a mutual rivalry for honour; and such men as these, when fighting side by side, one might almost consider able to make even a little band victorious over all the world. For a man in love would surely choose to have all the rest of the host rather than his favourite see him forsaking his station or flinging away his arms; sooner than this, he would prefer to die many deaths: while, as for leaving his favourite in the lurch, or not succouring him in his peril, no man is such a craven that Love's own influence cannot inspire him with a valour that makes him equal to the bravest born; and without doubt what Homer calls a 'fury inspired' by a god in certain heroes is the effect produced on lovers by Love's peculiar power. – PLATO, *SYMPOSIUM*

BELOW: **The classical Greek philosopher Plato agreed that loving couples make superior warriors.**

Plato and Plutarch therefore agreed that loving couples are of a benefit to a fighting force. This arises not only from their concern to protect the other against an attacking foe, but also not to shame themselves in front of their lover by showing cowardice on the battlefield.

In Homer, heterosexual love is to blame for most of the story's ills. It is the love between Paris and Helen that started the war; male ownership of the slave girls Chryseis and Briseis causes the quarrel between Achilles and Agamemnon. Critics of the idea that Achilles and Patroclus were lovers point to Achilles' relationship with Briseis as proof that he liked women. Homer himself tells us that Achilles and Patroclus slept apart from each other on separate sides of the tent with their slave girls. However, it is also true that, according to both Achilles and Agamemnon, female slaves were commodities to be swapped, changed and replaced. The love between Achilles and Patroclus, on the other hand, was irreplaceable; all Achilles wants, he says, after Patroclus' death, is to lie with him in his grave so they can be reunited once more.

Many ancient writers of the Archaic and Classical Greek period had no trouble accepting

TELEMACHUS AND PISISTRATUS

SOME SCHOLARS THINK ACHILLES and Patroclus were not the only gay couple in Homer. It has been proposed that in the *Odyssey* the warrior Telemachus and Pisistratus, the son of Nestor of Pylos, also have a homosexual liaison. In the book, Telemachus stops in at Pylos on his epic voyage to find his father, Odysseus, who is yet to return from Troy. In Pylos, Nestor puts Telemachus in the same bed as Pisistratus, who is at that time unmarried. Pisistratus then accompanies Telemachus on his journey and the two are found in Sparta in the same bed by Athena when she appears to Telemachus.

Critics of this theory say both Telemachus and Pisistratus are grown men, so therefore impossible to fit into the pederasty model. Both are too old to be an eromenos. But as we have seen, there is a great deal of evidence to prove the existence of homosexual relationships between grown men in the Greek military; trying to fit everything into the narrow bounds of the pederasty model is therefore futile.

It has been proposed that Telemachus, shown here, often shared a bed with Pisistratus in Homer's *Odyssey*.

the idea of homosexual love between Achilles and Patroclus. In Aeschylus' *Myrmidons*, Achilles falls into a fit of jealousy before Patroclus' corpse and accuses him of betraying their love by dying; Aeschines talks about the two warriors as lovers in his oration *Against Timarchus*; and one of Sophocles' lost plays was called *The Lovers of Achilles*.

The greatest matter of dispute among the ancient Greeks themselves appears to be whether or not Achilles was the erastes or the eromenos – an argument that has also been used in more recent times to discredit the idea that the relationship was homosexual. The writers Aeschines, Aeschylus and Athenaeus all believed the erastes must have been Achilles. However, in his *Symposium*, Plato suggests the erastes was Patroclus. This idea is reinforced by the famous Kylix by Sosias, which shows Achilles tending to Patroclus' wounds. On the cup Patroclus wears a beard, a sign of his older age.

Who was the erastes and who the eromenos, however, is a secondary matter that does not prove that Achilles and Patroclus were not lovers. In the *Iliad*, the union between Achilles and Patroclus and their separation through death is honoured by the gods. This is shown during the speech by Thetis, who knows that her son has not only lost the love of his life but is also one step closer to his own fate. It is a fate that neither Thetis nor any other god has the power to change.

ABOVE: **On this famous Kylix, Achilles binds Patroclus' wounds. The beard suggests that the older man in the relationship was not Achilles, but Patroclus.**

CHAPTER **6**

Gods, Men and Homer

The *Iliad* is a universe of gods and mortals. Homer's gods, however, are manipulative; they interfere endlessly in human affairs. Tales about the gods date from well before the invention of writing. But scholars still debate whether Homer was illiterate.

FROM HIS lofty position high on Mount Ida, Zeus watches the events of the Trojan War unfold. There has been high drama and tragedy on the battlefield. Under Zeus' watch, the Trojans have routed the Greeks. Hector and his men have pushed the Greeks back to the wooden palisade of their beach encampment. Here, full of adrenalin in his moment of *aristeia*, the Trojan lifts a boulder and hurls it through the gates:

Then brave Hector leaped inside with a face as dark as that of flying night. The gleaming bronze flashed fiercely about his body and he had two spears in his hand. None but a god could have withstood him as he flung himself into the gateway, and his eyes glared like fire. Then he turned round towards the Trojans and called on them to scale the wall, and they did as he bade them – some of them at once climbing over the wall, while others passed through the gates. – HOMER, *ILIAD*, BOOK XII

OPPOSITE: **In this Apotheosis of Homer, the poet is crowned by Time and the World, and acclaimed by all.**

OPPOSITE: **This bust depicts Zeus, the king of the Greek gods.**

These events are fated, for Zeus is generally the champion of the Trojans. The victory had also been achieved with divine intervention, as Zeus had 'given the greater glory to Hector' and the god Saturn had made the boulder lighter for the Trojan to hurl.

Such was the power of the Homeric gods, for their interference marked every moment of the war. The gods meddle from the start, causing the quarrel between Achilles and Agamemnon at the beginning of the poem:

So were the counsels of Jove [Zeus] fulfilled from the day on which the son of Atreus, king of men, and great Achilles, first fell out with one another. And which of the gods was it that set them on to quarrel? It was the son of Jove and Leto [Apollo]; for he was angry with the king and sent a pestilence upon the host to plague the people, because the son of Atreus had dishonoured Chryses his priest. – HOMER, *ILIAD*, BOOK I

BELOW: **This frieze of the gods comes from the Siphnian Treasury at Delphi, Greece.**

The focus of the *Iliad* is the war and the deeds of legendary figures, but behind each hero there is an individual god egging them on. The gods themselves have mixed motivations. Their agendas are sometimes based on family alliances, debts and favours; at other times a whim or a brainstorm. The gods eagerly watch the action in Troy from their lofty domain high on

Mount Olympus, a mountain range that sits between Macedonia and Greece. They live in unimaginable opulence inside their magnificent palace, which has been built by Hephaestus himself. However, they cannot tear themselves away from the Trojan War, and when their prodding from above is not enough they transform themselves into mortal form to intervene directly.

The Homeric gods are portrayed with human personalities. They can be loving, passionate and caring, but also petty, jealous, irrational and impulsive. On Olympus the gods fight, scold and punish each other like a mortal family: except they are not mortal and their immortality is never compromised by their actions on Earth.

At the head of the divine family is Zeus, the all-powerful 'father of gods and men'. When he enters the room in the palace 'the gods rose from their seats, before the coming of their sire. Not one of them dared to remain sitting, but all stood up as he came among them.'

> The Homeric gods are portrayed with human personalities. They can be loving and caring; but also petty, irrational and impulsive.

Zeus is also overwhelmingly the strongest of the gods; he cannot be overcome by force. When displeased, he is also willing to dole out punishments: he once strung his wife Hera from a tree with anvils hanging from her feet. Like many mortal couples, Hera and Zeus are often at odds. Hera, for example is a Greek sympathizer, while Zeus is for the Trojans.

Hera will do anything she can to destroy the Trojans, including subterfuge and sabotage. The goddess often tries to deceive Zeus to get her way. However, Zeus knows Hera's tricks and is not above reminding her of who is the dominant power: 'I mean to have it so; sit down and hold your tongue as I bid you for if I once begin to lay my hands about you, though all heaven were on your side it would profit you nothing.'

Zeus is serious, therefore, when in Book VIII he forbids Hera and the other Greek-loving gods from taking any further part in the war. This prohibition stays largely in force until Book XX, when a divine free-for-all breaks out. Before then, the events unfold supposedly without divine assistance. In this way, Zeus can carry out his intention for the Trojans to win the war.

Zeus is not the only god observing the Trojan successes on the battlefield. Watching from his perch on the island of Samothrace is Poseidon: god of the sea, 'lord of the earthquake', and Zeus' younger brother. Poseidon is on the side of the Greeks and in a bad mood with Zeus. He decides to lend a hand.

OPPOSITE: This fifth century BCE frieze from the Greek temple at Selinus, Sicily, depicts the first meeting between Zeus and Hera.

WHAT'S IN AN EPITHET?

HOMER AND HESIOD ARE the two poets who described the gods with formulaic epithets, short descriptions that define their skills, functions and appearance. Zeus is often the 'cloud gatherer', 'father of gods and men' and 'of the dazzling bolt'. Apollo is called 'son of Zeus', 'rouser of armies' and 'god of the silver bow'.

These epithets paint a picture of a god's abilities but probably also describe how people regarded them in Homer's day. Not all gods were thought of favourably. Ares, for example, is called by Homer the 'curse of men', 'sacker of cities' and 'of the glinting helmet'. Athena, by contrast, is the 'bright-eyed', 'tireless one' and 'hope of soldiers'.

Ares and Athena are both martial deities, but stand on opposite sides of the Trojan War. They are also polar opposites in terms of personality. Athena is the 'defender of cities' and known as a great protector, whereas Ares wants to destroy and is disliked by the other gods. His father Zeus tells Ares: 'Do not come whining here, Sir Facingbothways. I hate you worst of all the gods in Olympus, for you are ever fighting and making mischief. You have the intolerable and stubborn spirit of your mother.'

Ares' mother, Hera, is given the epithet 'cow-eyed' by Homer and knows deception is her best way to win over Zeus. She therefore enlists the help of Aphrodite, 'goddess of love', 'fair' and 'laughter-loving', to use her womanly wiles to seduce and then trick her husband. This would have the effect, as was her intention, of turning the tide of the war against the Greeks.

Right: This bust shows Hesiod, one of the earliest known Greek poets, alongside Homer.

His timing is good, as Zeus, who 'had thus brought Hector and the Trojans to the ships, he left them to their never-ending toil, and turned his keen eyes away, looking elsewhither... He no longer turned so much as a glance towards Troy, for he did not think that any of the immortals would go and help either Trojans or Danaans [Greeks].'

Poseidon uses this moment of Zeus' distraction to stride down from his lofty position and boost the morale of the assembled Greek warriors.

Morale is one of the elusive mysteries of the battlefield. Those whose morale is high can win the day armed only with sharp sticks, while fully armed militaries can fail through the lack of it. Homer commonly ascribes it to the influence of the gods: it comes as if from nowhere to fill warriors with a confidence and strength that was not previously there.

ABOVE: **Ares and Athena are here shown in combat with each other.**

ABOVE: This artwork shows Poseidon leaving the ocean to rally the Greeks and push the Trojans back.

This is what Poseidon gave to the Greek warriors as he strode out of the sea in mortal disguise and whispered into their ears to inspire them. His intervention is vital: the Greeks are holed up in their ships as the Trojans pile over the encampment wall towards them: 'Tears began falling from their eyes as they beheld them, for they made sure that they should not escape destruction; but the lord of the earthquake passed lightly about among them and urged their battalions to the front.'

Poseidon, however, is not brave enough to defend the Greeks openly; he fears that Zeus will see him. His morale building, however, is what keeps the Trojans from overrunning the Greek ships. One such Poseidon-inspired warrior is Idomeneus, who is 'thirsting for battle'.

Now when the Trojans saw Idomeneus coming on like a flame of fire, him and his squire clad in their richly wrought armour, they shouted and made towards him all in a body, and a furious hand-to-hand fight raged under the ships' sterns. Fierce as the shrill winds that whistle upon a day when dust lies deep on the roads, and the gusts raise it into a thick cloud – even such was the fury of the combat, and with might and main did they hack at each other with spear and sword throughout the host. The field bristled with the long and deadly spears which they bore. Dazzling was the sheen of their gleaming helmets, their fresh-burnished breastplates and glittering shields as they joined battle with one another. – HOMER, ILIAD, BOOK XIII

As battle rages on, the Greeks manage to push the Trojans back. But then there is another rout and the Trojans are upon them once more. This is a divine stalemate between Zeus and Poseidon and there can be no mortal victor. It is Zeus' will, however, that the Greeks will eventually prevail and that Achilles will be covered in glory. For this is what he promised Thetis, Achilles' mother. Poseidon, on the other hand, while too cunning to reveal himself on the battlefield, cannot win the day for the Trojans through morale building alone. Thus 'did these two devise a knot of war and battle, that none could unloose.'

The problem for the mortals playing out this proxy warfare on the actual battlefield is that there can be no conclusion; not until things are settled on Olympus. However, on Olympus there is no urgency, nor a sense that anything is wrong. The mortal world is where gods can play as they choose.

Given the gods' greater powers, do any of the mortals in the *Iliad* have any freedom over their own destinies, or is every action preordained or controlled by the gods? There are examples in the story of both things occurring. In Book I, for example,

Poseidon's intervention is vital for the Greeks, who are holed up in their ships as the Trojans pile over their encampment.

BELOW: Here, Zeus and Hera sit on their thrones on Mount Olympus, as Poseidon and Hermes seek an audience.

Athena stays Achilles' hand when he reaches for his sword to cut Agamemnon down. However, in book XI, Odysseus is left alone to make a decision about whether to retreat or stand his ground in battle. Although given no divine advice, he decides to stand and fight rather than be accused of cowardice. Later, Menelaus is also given the freedom to make a similar decision but chooses to run and not fight. However, although these examples show that some actions do not involve the gods, they are in the minority.

Whether assisted by the gods or not, the events on Earth have far graver repercussions than they do on Olympus. Achilles' falling out with Agamemnon and his subsequent withdrawal from the war has serious consequences that bring countless deaths on both sides. However, during an argument about the matter between Hera and Zeus, Hephaestus wonders whether the quarrel might ruin their dinner that night, and takes steps to defuse the argument by making a joke of it.

The point is that mortal decisions can have life and death consequences, but there are no fatal consequences for the immortals. If there is a dispute or disagreement, the gods can simply retreat back into their life of privilege on Olympus; the mortals cannot.

Meanwhile, back at Troy, the battle around the Greeks' beachhead encampment rages. However, Poseidon has rallied the Greeks to beat the Trojans back. His morale boosting has worked

BELOW: **The goddess Athena here looks down on the dispute between Achilles and Agamemnon.**

THE DECEPTION OF ZEUS

TO KEEP ZEUS' GAZE away from Troy, where Poseidon is helping the Greeks, Hera uses an aphrodisiac charm given to her by Aphrodite. Homer's description is reminiscent of warriors putting on their battle armour, and here Hera can be considered to be putting on hers. The scene would have been a great counterpoint to the long battle sequence that falls either side of it:

She [Hera] set herself to think how she might hoodwink him, and in the end she deemed that it would be best for her to go to Ida and array herself in rich attire, in the hope that Jove [Zeus] might become enamoured of her, and wish to embrace her. While he was thus engaged a sweet and careless sleep might be made to steal over his eyes and senses.

She went, therefore, to the room that her son Vulcan had made her, and the doors of which he had cunningly fastened by means of a secret key so that no other god could open them. Here she entered and closed the doors behind her. She cleansed all the dirt from her fair body with ambrosia, then she anointed herself with olive oil, ambrosial, very soft, and scented specially for herself – if it were so much as shaken in the bronze-floored house of Jove, the scent pervaded the universe of heaven and earth. With this she anointed her delicate skin, and then she plaited the fair ambrosial locks that flowed in a stream of golden tresses from her immortal head. She put on the wondrous robe which Minerva had worked for her...and she girded herself with a girdle that had a hundred tassels; then she fastened her earrings, three brilliant pendants that glistened most beautifully, through the pierced lobes of her ears, and threw a lovely new veil over her head.

– HOMER, *ILIAD*, BOOK XIV

This ninth century BCE statue of Hera comes from the Sanctuary of Hera, Argos, around 5 km from Mycenae.

and the Trojans have lost their opportunity to oust the Greeks permanently from their shores. The opposite of morale on the battlefield is panic, which now grips the Trojans as a resurgent Greek force arises.

In celebration, Poseidon lets out a loud cry with a 'voice that came from his deep chest [like] that of nine or ten thousand men when they are shouting in the thick of a fight.' This is dangerous, as it could catch the attention of Zeus, who is still looking elsewhere. To make sure he continues to be distracted, Hera carries out the celebrated seduction of her husband.

After she has prepared her womanly wiles, Hera visits Zeus on Mount Ida; he, of course, cannot resist her. But she asks that he throw a cloud around them so they cannot be seen, and in this mischief Zeus cuts himself off from the retreating Trojans below. After their lovemaking, Zeus falls into a deep sleep. Hera has scored a great victory against her husband; the fate of Troy now hangs in the balance.

Gods and Men

As Zeus sleeps in the clouds, the warriors of the plain inflict pain and death upon one another. Zeus's post-coital doze occurs during a murderous slaughter below, once again showing the gulf between the two worlds. Hector has previously been told by Iris that Zeus will 'vouchsafe you strength to slay till you reach the ships, and till night falls at the going down of the sun.' But now he has been savagely beaten back. What then is the will of the gods and how will his destiny reveal itself?

As the readers of the *Iliad*, we already know Hector's fate, as Homer has pre-warned us of it. Zeus has promised Thetis that her son Achilles will be brought immortal glory, and this honour means that Hector will die. When this comes, Hector realizes he has been abandoned by the gods to face his demise alone: 'Minerva [Athena] has inveigled me; death is now indeed exceedingly near at hand and there is no way out of it – for so Jove [Zeus] and his son Apollo the far-darter have willed it, though heretofore they have been ever ready to protect me. My doom has come upon me.'

OPPOSITE: **This Roman fresco from Pompeii shows the marriage between Hera and Zeus.**

The gods, then, are deceptive and callous. Although their power over a mortal's final destiny is unclear, they seem to be able to choose when they live or die. Aphrodite, for example, plucks Paris from his duel with Menelaus and denies the jilted Greek his prize. When Helen chastises Paris and tells him Menelaus is the better warrior, Paris interjects: 'Wife, do not vex me with your reproaches. This time, with the help of Minerva [Athena], Menelaus has vanquished me; another time I may myself be victor, for I too have gods that will stand by me.'

Athena is another great saver of lives during battle. When called upon by the injured Diomedes, Athena heals his wounds and takes away the veil that stops men from seeing the gods. This means Diomedes can see which gods are helping and which are not.

Most mortals, of course, live in ignorance of the gods while still hoping for divine favour. Mortals pray to the gods, make offerings and try to stay on their best side – but, as we have seen, they are wholly at their mercy. Only the bravest warriors battle against their fate, but they know they are powerless to change it.

While the gods have the power to pluck their favourite individuals from the battlefield, do they have the power to change fate itself? If any of the gods are able to change fate it is Zeus. However, it is unclear if events are predestined and beyond even Zeus' control. For example, Zeus can predict the deaths of heroes such as Achilles and Patroclus, but also worries that Achilles may be capable of undoing fate itself. This moment of doubt comes at the same time as Zeus decides to amend his prohibition on the gods to join the fighting at Troy. Now, he commands them to take part:

I shall stay here seated on Mt. Olympus and look on in peace, but

BELOW: **A statue of Athena, goddess of war.**

do you others go about among Trojans and Achaeans, and help either side as you may be severally disposed. If Achilles fights the Trojans without hindrance they will make no stand against him; they have ever trembled at the sight of him, and now that he is roused to such fury about his comrade, he will override fate itself and storm their city.

– HOMER, *ILIAD*, BOOK XX

The concept that Achilles could 'override fate itself' implies that nothing is certain, that destiny is fluid and can be changed by human will. Zeus also hints at this when his son Sarpedon nears his own fate, death at the hands of Patroclus. He complains about this to Hera and tells her he is considering sparing Sarpedon. Hera, always careful not to provoke her husband, reminds him that the choice is his, but it is also his duty not to change fate.

ABOVE: An illustration of the dead Sarpedon, son of Zeus, who Hera does not let him spare.

Do as you will, but we shall not all of us be of your mind. I say further, and lay my saying to your heart, that if you send Sarpedon safely to his own home, some other of the gods will be also wanting to escort his son out of battle, for there are many sons of gods fighting round the city of Troy, and you will make every one jealous. If, however, you are fond of him and pity him, let him indeed fall by the hand of Patroclus, but as soon as the life is gone out of him, send Death and sweet Sleep to bear him off the field and take him to the broad lands of Lycia, where his brothers and his kinsmen will bury him with mound and pillar,

ABOVE: A marble fragment from Apulia, Italy, showing a battle between the Greeks and Trojans.

in due honour to the dead.' The sire of gods and men assented, but he shed a rain of blood upon the earth in honour of his son whom Patroclus was about to kill on the rich plain of Troy far from his home. – HOMER, *ILIAD*, BOOK XVI

So fate can be changed, but it is up to the gods to make sure it is not, otherwise the natural order may be upset. Perhaps this would mean chaos would descend and a great war between the gods would rage. This is an unthinkable prospect if caused by a quarrel over mere mortals.

In the end, Zeus, suitably chastised by Hera, lets Sarpedon be slain and events are left to follow their fated course. However, under Zeus' orders, the gods gleefully join the fray to fight each other vicariously through their chosen warriors. For the gods

this is a last hurrah before Hector is slain and the siege comes
to an end. The triumph and tragedy can be played out with
abandon and excess – there are no consequences for those who
dwell on Olympus.

For the fighting mortals themselves, there is the hope that a
divine presence may single them out and shine down on them.
This is the best the warriors can hope for. It is this hope that
keeps them battling through seemingly impossible odds; without
divinity, the battlefield is otherwise a place too brutal and
meaningless to comprehend.

Enter the Bard

The warriors on the plain of Troy are not the only mortals to call
upon the gods for help: the bards, the singers of the stories of
war and men, also do this. In the *Odyssey*, the bard Demodocus
calls on the muse to help him tell his tales. Demodocus is an
important figure in Homeric legend, a bard 'whom the muse had
dearly loved, but to whom she had given both good and evil, for
though she had endowed him with a divine gift of song, she had
robbed him of his eyesight.'

BELOW: Here Odysseus
weeps as the blind bard
Demodocus recounts the
story of the fall of Troy.

ABOVE: **A Greek poet, probaby meant to be Homer, recites to a group of Greeks in this idealised view of Ancient Greek life.**

of hexameter verse that make up the *Iliad*, for example, were probably composed in the eighth century BCE and have therefore survived more than 2700 years. How did this happen?

The Greek historian Herodotus tells us that Homer lived around 400 years previously, some time in the ninth century. The ancient scholar of Homer, Aristarchus of Samothrace, thought that Homer had existed around 140 years after the Trojan War took place. This would place Homer sometime around 1100 BCE. Both men agreed that Homer was blind. If Homer did indeed live in the period theorized by Aristarchus, it would have been during the Dark Age of the Mediterranean and Near East.

Before this Bronze Age collapse, the two written languages most available to Homer would have been the Mycenaean Linear B and Hittite cuneiform, but both languages disappeared with the kingdoms themselves.

No one is exactly sure where Homer lived, although many suggest it was somewhere in western Anatolia, modern-day Turkey. The ancient Greek city of Smyrna is one possible location; the small island of Chios is another. It is most likely that

Homer, whether he had some access to the written word or not, performed his poems orally. The poems of the epic cycle of Troy were handed down from one bard to another over centuries. They became in a sense committed to collective memory.

It was centuries before the poems were written down. It is indeed possible that the story of the Trojan War was told to a bard by someone who was actually there at the time, or knew someone who was.

Oral poetry is common among many cultures, from the Maori to the Vikings. Poetry was recited or sung aeons before it was written down. Sometimes these oral traditions have continued till modern times, including in twentieth-century Yugoslavia, Armenia and Ireland.

This oral tradition typically uses 'formulas' or familiar epithets as handy set phrases that will fit the meter and fill in time while the poet decides how to continue their improvised song. That is why later, when the poems are set down on paper, the formulaic epithets form such an important part of the work.

Homer, whether he had some access to the written word or not, performed his poems orally.

BELOW: Nestor's famous cup. Using the new Greek alphabet it reads: 'I am Nestor's cup, good to drink from.'

However, many believe that Homer must have used some form of writing in his composition, even if he did not write the poems down himself but dictated them to a scribe. Perhaps we will never know. Homer remains mysterious.

It is thought the *Iliad* was first written down sometime around 750–725 BCE, probably on Egyptian papyrus or animal skins; Herodotus says that the fifth-century Greeks used the word for 'skin' when talking about books. One is also reminded

THE WRITTEN WORD

THERE IS ALMOST NO evidence to suggest that the characters in the *Iliad* or *Odyssey* knew how to read or write. In the *Iliad*, writing has only one obscure mention, in a side story in Book VI that is largely irrelevant to the main tale:

'The king was angered, but shrank from killing Bellerophon, so he sent him to Lycia with lying letters of introduction, written on a folded tablet, and containing much ill against the bearer. He bade Bellerophon show these letters to his father-in-law, to the end that he might thus perish.'

We don't know what written language was used in Bellerophon's letter of introduction, but it is likely to have been Linear B, the Mycenaean script of more than 200 signs and symbols that only trained scribes could use. Linear B was lost after the Bronze Age collapse and for a time the world around the Mediterranean was largely illiterate. What re-emerged was a Greek alphabet of fewer than 30 letters that could be used to write poetry. Amazing as it seems, this alphabet was gifted to the Greeks by the great traders of the Mediterranean, the Phoenicians. The Phoenicians were a Semitic trading people whose main bases were the Palestine cities of Tyre and Sidon. Phoenician merchants kept up a booming business during the Dark Age and their ships were known in most ports around the Mediterranean.

The Phoenicians also travelled to the island of Pithekoussai, today's Ischia in Italy's Bay of Naples, to exploit its iron, silver and tin. Here, too, were the Greek survivors of the Dark Age; somehow the two ended up as partners. Here, their language was also traded. The Phoenician alphabet was made up only of consonants and used mainly for the purposes of trade and business; the Greeks added five vowels and turned it into a language that could be used for poetry and prose.

The great archaeological evidence for the new Greek alphabet was the 'Cup of Nestor', a pottery drinking cup dating from the eighth century BCE. Scratched

of Bellerophon's letter of introduction, 'written on a folded tablet'. Whatever material the words were written on, the actual construction of the poem would have taken an extremely long time. The early Greek alphabet used for the poem on Nestor's Cup was crude and unwieldy; it would take years to perfect a written copy of a carefully thought out spoken poem.

By the sixth century BCE, Homer's poems were in circulation around the Classical world of Greece, by now written out on

into the side in the new Greek alphabet is this poem:

'I am Nestor's cup good to drink from. Whoever drinks this cup empty,

Straight away desire for beautiful-crowned Aphrodite will seize him.'

With this new alphabet, Homer's epics could be written down for the first time.

Here, Phoenician traders are shown peddling their wares in a Mediterranean port.

ABOVE: This sixth century BCE ostrakon has an ink inscription with lines from Homer's Iliad.

large papyrus rolls. This was the form known to the scholars of Homer in Alexandria, the Egyptian city founded by Alexander the Great in the fourth century BCE. Here, it is highly likely that Aristarchus of Samothrace, a resident scholar at the library of Alexandria, divided the poem up into its 24 books. This would have been a purely pragmatic process, as papyrus had a tendency to break if the rolls were physically too long.

Over the centuries, parchment replaced papyrus, but the tradition of copying out Homer's poems by hand remained. After the collapse of the Roman Empire, parchment copies of the *Iliad* could be found in parts of Western Europe such as Italy as late as the fourteenth century CE. Unfortunately, no one could read them. Knowledge of Greek in Western Europe had been lost and was revived by Greek-speaking scholars fleeing from Byzantium after it fell to the Ottoman Empire in 1453. With the language came many Greek manuscripts from antiquity, including Homer's poems.

First Edition

The first printed edition of the *Iliad* was published in 1588 in Florence, which began the long tradition of Homer in print that is still running strong today. His poems are considered the oldest works of literature in the world and an entire field of academia involves itself with the analysis of his texts.

Homer the man, the Trojan War and the relationship of the poems to history have fascinated people for nearly 3000 years. Yet it is the magic of the texts themselves that has sustained this fascination. The earliest of the world's great writers also remains perhaps the greatest. Homer casts the longest and largest shadow.

OPPOSITE: The title page from a 1616 edition of Homer's works.

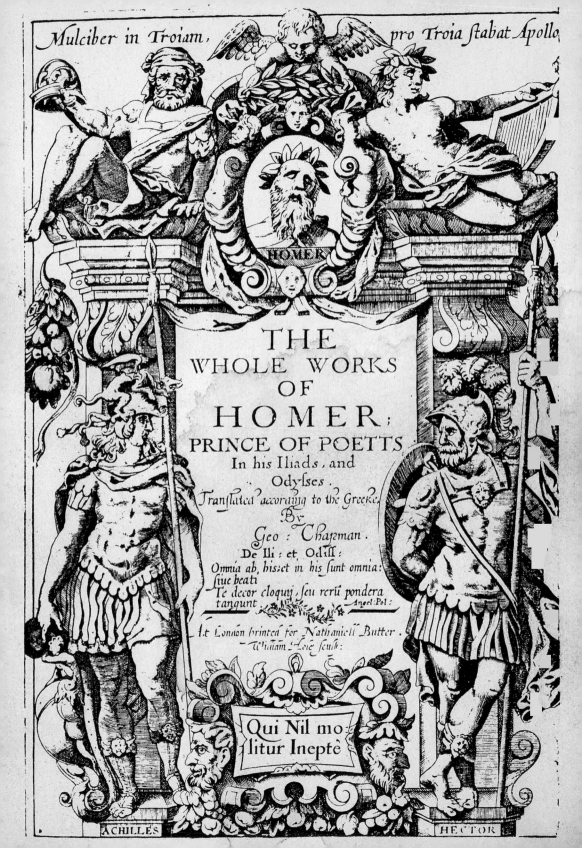

Mulciber in Troiam, pro Troia stabat Apollo

HOMER

THE
WHOLE WORKS
OF
HOMER;
PRINCE OF POETTS
In his Iliads, and
Odysses.
Translated according to the Greeke.
By
Geo: Chapman.

De Ili: et Odiss:
Omnia ab, his:et in his sunt omnia:
siue beati
Te decor eloquij, seu rerú pondera
tangunt   Angel:Pol:

At London printed for Nathaniell Butter.
William Hole sculp:

Qui Nil mo
litur Inepte

ACHILLES   HECTOR

CHAPTER 7

New Civilizations from Old

It is Aeneas who recounts the sacking of Troy to a hushed audience in Virgil's epic poem. The Trojans' fate was to be the same as many real Bronze Age refugees, whose cities fell to earthquake, famine and barbarian attack.

I N VIRGIL's *Aeneid*, Aeneas is the Trojan warrior who will lead the survivors of Troy to found a new civilization: Rome. In the hall of Dido, queen of Carthage in North Africa, Aeneas tells the terrible details of Troy's destruction. He describes the wooden horse built by Odysseus and left at the deserted Greek camp. Inside the horse is a company of the Greeks' 'picked soldiery, crowding the vaulted caverns in the dark – the horse's belly – with men fully armed.'

The Trojans gaze at the wooden horse and ponder its meaning. The warrior Thymoetes shouts that the horse is a prize and should be hauled into the city, but others suspect it is a trap; drag it into the sea, cut it open, or set it alight, the city elders say. Then the priest Laocoon comes running from the city and cries at the crowd:

'O my poor people, Men of Troy, what madness has come over you? / Can you believe the enemy truly gone? / A gift from

OPPOSITE: **A depiction of the horse that brought down Troy. It is not in Homer's *Iliad* that we learn the details of the city's fall, but rather Virgil's Aeneid.**

the Danaans, and no ruse? / Is that Ulysses' way, as you have known him? / Achaeans must be hiding in this timber, / Or it was built to butt against our walls, / Peer over them into our houses, pelt / The city from the sky. Some crookedness / Is in this thing. Have no faith in the horse! / Whatever it is, even when Greeks bring gifts / I fear them, gifts and all.' – VIRGIL, *AENEID*, BOOK II

Laocoon then grabs a spear and hurls it at the belly of the horse, but the weapon finds no human purchase. Instead, the Trojans' attention is diverted by the appearance of the villain, Sinon, a Greek who explains he was left behind with the horse as an offering to the goddess Athena. Athena, Sinon explains, had cursed the Greeks after Odysseus desecrated one of her temples. To appease her, the wooden horse had been built as an offering so they could leave Troy and be guaranteed safe passage home. Sinon warns that if any harm came to the statue, Athena would destroy Troy. However, if the horse were taken inside the city walls then the Trojans would be guaranteed Athena's help in defeating the Greeks in a future war.

Suddenly, as if to confirm the divine providence of Sinon's account, two serpents 'coiling, uncoiling, swam abreast for shore, their underbellies showing as their crests reared red as blood above the swell swam through the sea for shore.' The snakes devour Laocoon's two sons before choking the priest to death, and then slither away to sit at the shrine of Athena.

Word quickly spread that Laocoon had paid for profaning the horse – and therefore Athena – with his spear. 'The offering must be hauled to its true home,' the crowd chants, and the Trojan horse 'deadly, pregnant with enemies' was pulled inside the city walls. Then, as the city slept, Sinon frees the Greek warriors from the horse. The death knell for Troy had sounded.

ABOVE: **A bust of Aeneas: the Trojan who founded Rome and whose progeny allegedly went on to colonize several other countries.**

Meanwhile, the ghost of the fallen Hector appears before Aeneas in a dream. The Trojan prince no longer has the immaculate body that the gods famously preserved against Achilles' brutal desecrations. Now it is 'gaunt with sorrow, streaming tears, all torn – as if by the violent car on his death day – and black with bloody dust, his puffed-out feet cut by the rawhide thongs.'

It is this apparition of Hector that tells Aeneas to flee Troy, for the city is now doomed. Instead, Hector explains, Aeneas' destiny is to take the survivors of Troy and 'find for them the great walls that one day you'll dictate, when you have roamed the sea.' Aeneas does not heed Hector's words as he awakes to the commotion of the Greek attack around him; he dons his armour and runs to the defence of the city.

BELOW: This eighteenth century painting shows Aeneas at the court of Dido, Queen of Carthage.

But Aeneas' efforts are in vain, as the freshly returned Greek army are let into the city and begin their slaughter. Aeneas details the horror of the sacking, but the most pitiful moment is the death of Priam, the city's elderly king:

When he [Priam] saw his city stormed and seized, his gates / wrenched apart the enemy camped in his palace depths / the old man dons his armor long unused, he clamps it / round his

shoulders shaking with age and, / all for nothing, / straps his useless sword to his hip, then makes / for the thick of battle, out to meet his death…Suddenly, / look, a son of Priam, Polites, just escaped / from slaughter at Pyrrhus' hands, comes racing in / through spears, through enemy fighters, fleeing down / the long arcades and deserted hallways – badly wounded, / Pyrrhus hot on his heels, a weapon poised for the kill, / about to seize him, about to run him through and pressing home as Polites reaches his parents and collapses, / vomiting out his lifeblood before their eyes. / At that, Priam, trapped in the grip of death, not holding back, not checking his words, his rage: / 'You!' he cries, 'you and your vicious crimes! / If any power on high recoils at such an outrage, / let the gods

repay you for all your reckless work, / grant you the thanks, the rich reward you've earned. / You've made me see my son's death with my own eyes, / defiled a father's sight with a son's lifeblood. / You say you're Achilles' son? You lie! Achilles / never treated his enemy Priam so. No, he honored / a suppliant's rights, he blushed to betray my trust, / he restored my Hector's bloodless corpse for burial, / sent me safely home to the land I rule!' / With that / and with all his might the old man flings his spear – / but too impotent now to pierce, it merely grazes / Pyrrhus' brazen shield that blocks its way / and clings there, dangling limp from the boss, / all for nothing. Pyrrhus shouts back: 'Well then, / down you go, a messenger to my father, Peleus' son! / Tell him about my vicious work, how Neoptolemus / degrades his father's name – don't you forget. / Now – die!' / That said, he drags the old man / straight to the altar, quaking, slithering on through /*

ABOVE: Here the horse is taken inside the gates of Troy, the fate of the city now sealed.

OPPOSITE: The Trojan Laocoon and his sons are strangled by sea serpents. It was taken as a divine portent that the horse should be transported into Troy.

slicks of his son's blood, and twisting Priam's hair / in his left hand, his right hand sweeping forth his sword – / a flash of steel – he buries it hilt-deep in the king's flank. – VIRGIL, *AENEID*, BOOK II

As Priam is killed, Aeneas thinks of his own father, wife Creusa and son Iulus left waiting at his home. Realizing he must leave the city with his family he races back to save them, but as they all try to escape Creusa is lost. Then, as Aeneas scours the burning city for her, Creusa's ghost appears before him. She tells him that he will land near the Tiber and start his new kingdom with a queen by his side. Then, Aeneas laments: 'with this she left me weeping, wishing that I could say so many things and faded on the tenuous air. Three times I tried to put my arms around her neck, three times enfolded nothing...'

The devastation complete, Aeneas joins his father and son safe outside the burning city. With them are gathered a crowd of refugees – the last remaining survivors. These are the Trojans who will, according to legend, go on to found the city of Rome. However, before then, Virgil's mythical Trojans would join the wandering exiles of the real Bronze Age; the fate of Troy would also beset the kingdoms of Hatti and Mycenae, as their once great civilizations fell in flames.

The Collapse of Mycenae

The sack of Troy was the great prize the warriors of the *Iliad* had sought for over a decade, but the victory was bitter. Many of the Greek heroes would meet terrible deaths. Their leader, Agamemnon, the king of the city-state of Mycenae, would be murdered by his wife's lover. Like Aeneas, Agamemnon's fate in some ways mirrored the historical reality, for the real city-state of Mycenae was destroyed by violence and fire and the other Mycenaean city-states would follow. However, the destruction of Mycenaean Greece was only one part of a catastrophe that swept away the civilizations of the Mediterranean and Near East. The Bronze Age ended in ruin.

BELOW: On this Classical Greek vase, Aeneas is shown carrying his father Anchises from the burning city of Troy.

The widespread destruction of the Bronze Age collapse was immediately followed by a period sometimes called the Greek Dark Age. During this time, the Mycenaean palaces were abandoned, writing systems were forgotten, long-distance trade and diplomacy ended, government and religious bureaucracies ceased to exist; the people of Greece returned to a simple, pastoral lifestyle.

How could such a catastrophe have beset imperial Mycenae, one of the great superpowers of the day?

AGAMEMNON'S END

RULER OF MYCENAE'S MIGHTIEST city-state and leader of the Greek foray to retrieve Helen, Agamemnon should have returned from Troy to a life of fame and luxury. Instead, his fate is revealed to Odysseus, who travels to the 'land of the dead' during his *Odyssey*. To attract the spirits of the dead, Odysseus must dig a trench and fill it with ram's blood; the ghosts of the dead must drink the blood to regain their voice. The spirit of Agamemnon thus reveals that he was killed at the hand of his wife Clytemnestra and her lover Aegisthus:

'Aegisthus and my wicked wife were the death of me between them. He asked me to his house, feasted me, and then butchered me most miserably as though I were a fat beast in a slaughter house, while all around me my comrades were slain like sheep or pigs…I heard Priam's daughter Cassandra scream as Clytemnestra killed her close beside me. I lay dying upon the earth with the sword in my body, and raised my hands to kill the slut of a murderess…' – HOMER, ODYSSEY, BOOK XI

While he is talking to Agamemnon, the spirit of Achilles also appears before Odysseus and speaks to him: 'What daring brought you down to the House of Death?' Achilles reveals the true horror of the underworld and the ignorance of the living about eternity: 'By god, I'd rather slave on earth for another man, some dirt-poor farmer who scrapes to keep alive, than rule down here over all the breathless dead.'

This illustration of the murder of Agamemnon shows Clytemnestra standing unrepentantly with an axe.

ABOVE: **The ruins of the once great city-state of Mycenae are shown here as they are today.**

Here much remains mysterious. Illiteracy prevailed and there were no scribes to record the downfall. The Hittites left none of the cuneiform tablets that have revealed so much about the age of Troy. The evidence is fragmentary and difficult, but seems to suggest that the collapse had many causes.

What we know is that during the thirteenth century BCE, the trade routes of the Mediterranean and Near East became unstable and their civilizations fell under increasing threat of attack. In response, the city-states of Mycenae began large defensive works, especially around coastal areas; it was clear an invasion was expected to come from the sea.

In the city-states of Tiryns and Mycenae, massive 'cyclopean' walls constructed from limestone boulders were built around the cities; some were up to 7m (23ft) thick. Tiryns 'of the high walls', as Homer called it, also added long underground tunnels that could be used as a last refuge during a siege. Both Tiryns and Mycenae constructed complex waterworks to ensure their water supply should not be cut off. In Orchomenos, a mile-long wall was built around the agricultural land that surrounded the city.

Elsewhere in Greece, similar fortifications were constructed: in Corinth, Araxos and Lakonia, cyclopean walls were built

ABOVE: The great 'Cyclopean' walls of Tiryns are still standing, despite the ancient devastation wrought upon it.

facing the sea – and they still stand today. However, the walls were not strong enough to withstand whatever their Mycenaean inhabitants feared would overrun them.

Sea Raiders

The preparations against an invasion by sea are recorded in the only written documentary evidence from the time – Linear B tablets found at the palace of Pylos. One tablet is tellingly titled: 'Thus the watchers are guarding the coasts'. This is a roll call of the local military heads protecting the city and the numbers of men under their command: 'Command of Maleus at Owitono: Ampelitawon, Orestas, Etewas, Kokkion... Fifty suwerowijo men of Owitono at Oikhalia... Ten Kuparissian kekide men at Aithalewes... Thirty men from Oikhalia to Owitohno.'

Unlike Mycenae and Tiryns, Pylos never saw the need for high cyclopean defences, such was the confidence in its own army. But it too was to experience fear and panic in its later days, as the palace hurriedly requested warriors to protect it; a force of around 1500 warriors was quickly assembled. An atmosphere of last-ditch panic, of desperate defensive measures, is seen in another Linear B tablet from Pylos. Human sacrifices, rarely seen before, are now made to appease the Mycenaean gods.

PYLOS: perform a certain action at the shrine of Poseidon and…the town, and bring the gifts and bring those to carry them. One gold cup, two women…PYLOS: perform a certain action at the shrines of the Dove-goddess and of Iphemedeia and of Diwja, and bring the gifts and bring those to carry them. To the Dove goddess: one gold bowl, one woman. To Iphemedeia: one gold bowl. To Diwja: one gold bowl, one woman. To Hermes… one gold cup, one man. PYLOS: perform a certain action at the shrine of Zeus, and bring the gifts and bring those to carry them. To Zeus: one gold bowl, one man. To Hera: one gold bowl, one woman. To Drimios the priest of Zeus: one gold bowl, one man.

— PYLOS LINEAR B TABLET

More dramatically still, this last Linear B sentence trails off the edge of the tablet, as if the scribe was interrupted in his writing at the exact moment the city was overrun. There was

BELOW: The legendary tablets of Pylos were found inside the ruins of the palace. Much of what we know about the Mycenaeans comes from these tablets.

certainly not time to fire the tablet in a kiln; it was baked hard in the flames that engulfed the city. Nor were any human remains found during excavations of the site, and we must assume the city was attacked, sacked and its people enslaved: the Greeks suffered the annihilation they had inflicted on Troy.

This time the attackers were the mysterious Sea Peoples, a marauding coalition of warriors and their families who united to attack the established civilizations of the Mediterranean and Near East. The army that sacked Pylos was certainly not merely a group of opportunistic warriors out on random raids; instead it appears to have been a well-organized force with a plan to bring down one Mycenaean city after another.

Earthquakes struck both Myceane and Tiryns at about the same time. Greece also suffered bad harvests and famine, and overpopulation affected much of the wider Mediterranean and

BELOW: This clay coffin lid from the Middle East provides a likeness of one of the Sea Peoples.

Near East. Together, these elements made many civilizations increasingly vulnerable; many city dwellers ended up as refugees. Some of these displaced people may well have joined the Sea Peoples grouping to attack other cities.

Agamemnon's Mycenae, bursting with booty from a recently plundered Troy, must have been a tempting target, especially if the city's defences had been compromised by an earthquake. Whoever was left among the proud warriors of Mycenae rode out to meet the invaders. However, equipped with new lightweight armour and long swords, the attackers made short work of the Mycenaean chariots. The Mycenaeans were defeated, the citadel overrun, and its people enslaved, just as Pylos had been.

> We must assume the city was attacked, sacked and its people enslaved: the Greeks suffered the annihilation they had inflicted on Troy.

One city-state after another was destroyed by fire: Krisa, Menelaion, Araxos, Orchomenos and Thebes. Most of these citadels would be abandoned for good; Pylos, Krisa and Menelaion were never occupied again. Others, such as Mycenae and Tiryns, found a kind of survival as people returned to the ruined cities and rebuilt shanty towns inside their cyclopean walls, but the power of the kings was gone.

Mycenae limped on in this way for decades until another party of invaders delivered the death blow, ransacking the city and enslaving its people. Homer's great age of heroes was over.

The Sea Peoples in Egypt

Not all civilizations fell during the Bronze Age collapse: Ancient Egypt was twice able to defeat the Sea Peoples and survive for several hundred years afterwards. As the Egyptians lived to tell the tale, they also recorded their encounters. The reign of Ramses II contains the earliest Egyptian reference to the Sea Peoples, inscribed on the Tanis and Aswan Stelae.

The inscriptions describe a 1290 BCE battle between Ramses II and an attacking army that included the 'unruly Sherden whom no one had ever known how to combat; they came boldly sailing in their warships from the midst of the sea, none being able to withstand them.' The ensuing battle took place in the Nile Delta and was won by Ramses, who 'destroyed the warriors of the Great Green sea.' It is interesting to note that Ramses then incorporated many captured Sherden warriors in his subsequent 1274 Battle of Kadesh against the Hittites. This was the Hittites' first encounter with the Sea Peoples, but it would not be their last.

The Sea Peoples once again attacked Egypt in 1210 BCE. The son of Ramses, Pharaoh Merneptah, describes an attack by

WHO WERE THE SEA PEOPLES?

SCHOLARS STILL ARGUE ABOUT the identity of these elusive and largely undocumented figures. Their name comes from the Egyptians, who were among their victims. The Egyptians name the Sea Peoples as the Denyen, Peleset, Shekelesh, Sherden, Teresh, Tjekker, Weshesh, Karkisha, Lukka, Tursha and Akawasha: they came from Anatolia, Syria, Cyprus, Palestine, Phoenicia, Sardinia, Sicily and Greece. It has been proposed that the Akawasha were from Mycenae itself and it is difficult not to compare the name with that given to the Greeks by Homer: the Achaiwoi. Is it possible that disaffected Mycenaean warriors therefore joined the Sea Peoples in search of loot and new lands after the fall of their own city-states?

Depictions of the Sea Peoples on Egyptian bas reliefs show similar weaponry and armour to that of the Mycenaeans, among others. However, it is also known that the Sea Peoples were equipped with new weapons that included small round shields, light throwing spears, and long swords for thrusting and cutting. Some of these swords were made of the material that would dominate the new age and make bronze obsolete: iron.

Armed with the breakthrough weaponry, the Sea Peoples sailed around the civilizations of the eastern Mediterranean and Near East, raiding and destroying. Part of the mystery is their motive: was it for loot and slaves, or was there a more pressing issue driving them? In many cases, the Sea Peoples are recorded as travelling with women and children, implying that they were migrants on the move, quite possibly refugees uprooted by trouble or destruction in their own homelands. Some of the Sea Peoples, however, were simply pirates. The Lukka from Anatolia, for example, frequently made raids on Cyprus and Phoenicia.

In fact, the Sea Peoples might have included different groups at different times with different aims. The uniting factor is their deadly efficiency: only the might of Egypt was capable of withstanding them.

the neighbouring Libyans and their allies, who included the Lukka, Sherden, Shekelesh and 'Akawasha-people of the foreign lands of the sea.'

Merneptah's account, recorded in an inscription, says: 'The wretched, fallen chief of Libya, Meryey, has fallen upon the country with his bowmen – Sherden, Shekelesh, Akawasha, Lukka, Teresh, taking the best of every warrior and every man of war of his country. He has brought his wife and his children – leaders of the camp, and he has reached the western boundary.'

Despite being caught off guard by the attack, Merneptah repelled the invaders in one day and killed over six thousand of their warriors – or so the pharaoh says. Merneptah reports the army of the Sea Peoples included women, children, oxen and wagons, implying again that the attackers were migrants on the move rather than mere raiders. Some of the 9500 prisoners captured during the battle included civilians as well as soldiers; were some of these also Mycenaean refugees?

The final attack by the Sea Peoples occurred a generation later, during the reign of Ramses III. We know much about this conflict from the inscriptions and images left on the relief of the Pharaoh's Great Temple at Medinet Habu. Here, the pharaoh describes the Sea Peoples: 'the foreign countries made a conspiracy in their islands. All at once the lands were on the move, scattered in war. No country could stand before their

ABOVE: The Tanis Stelae of Ramses II gives the earliest ever Egyptian reference to the Sea Peoples.

RIGHT: Ramses III is shown here defeating the Sea Peoples with 'warships, galleys and barges manned from bow to stern with valiant warriors'.

arms. Hatti, Kode, Carchemish, Arzawa, Alashia: they were cut off.' The inscription continues:

They came with fire prepared before them, forward to Egypt. Their main support was Peleset, Tjekker, Shekelesh, Denyen, and Weshesh. Their lands were united, and they laid their hands upon the land as far as the Circle of the Earth. Their hearts were confident, full of their plans. Now, it happened through this god, the lord of gods, that I was prepared and armed to trap them like wild fowl. He furnished my strength and caused my plans to prosper. I went forth, directing these marvellous things. I equipped my frontier in Zahi, prepared before them. The chiefs, the captains of infantry, the nobles, I caused to equip the river-mouths, like a strong wall, with warships, galleys, and barges. They were manned from bow to stern with valiant warriors bearing their arms, soldiers of all the choicest of Egypt, being like lions roaring upon the mountain-tops. The charioteers were warriors, and all good officers, ready of hand. Their horses were quivering in their every limb, ready to crush the countries under their feet. I, King Ramses III, was made a far-striding hero, conscious of his might, valiant to lead his army in the day of battle. – RAMSES III, INSCRIPTION AT MEDINET HABU

What followed were two battles, one at land and one at sea. The images on the relief at Medinet Habu suggest the invaders were ambushed, for they are shown on a confused and chaotic battlefield with women, children and oxen all caught up in the fray. Ramses used his chariots to deadly effect by driving them into the heart of the melee: the enemy was easily defeated. Battle by sea ended in an even greater victory, as the Sea Peoples were trapped in their boats, which were then capsized. Ramses III describes the action:

BELOW: This bas relief from the Medinet Habu Temple at Luxor, Egypt, shows the Sea Peoples defeated by Ramses III.

Those who reached my boundary, their seed is not; their heart and their soul are finished forever and ever. As for those who

had assembled before them on the sea, the full flame was in their front, before the river-mouths, and a wall of metal upon the shore surrounded them. They were dragged, overturned, and laid low upon the beach; slain and made heaps from stern to bow of their galleys, while all their things were cast upon the water. I turned back the waters to remember Egypt; when they mention my name in their land, may it consume them, while I sit upon the throne of Harakhte, and the serpent-diadem is fixed upon my head, like Re. I permit not the countries to see the boundaries of Egypt… As for the Nine Bows, I have taken away their land and their boundaries; they are added to mine. Their chiefs and their people come to me with praise.

— RAMSES III, INSCRIPTION AT MEDINET HABU

BELOW: **Ramses III is shown here on his mortuary temple of Medinet Habu, Luxor, Egypt.**

The chiefs not prostrating themselves before Ramses with praise were summarily executed; leaders from each different country involved in the attack were made an example of in this

AMMURAPI'S TABLETS

LIKE THE LINEAR B tablets of Pylos, King Ammurapi of Ugarit's tablets lay unsent in the city's kiln. They were not baked there, however, but instead by the fire that razed his city to the ground. Ammurapi's last correspondence from the tablets says:

My father, the king of Alashia, behold, the enemy ships came here, my cities were burned, and they did evil things to my country. Does not my father know that all my troops and chariots are in the Hittite country, and all my ships are in the land of Lycia?... Thus the country is abandoned to itself. May my father know it: the seven ships of the enemy that came here inflicted much damage upon us when thy servant delivered thy word to me... The enemy advances against us and there is no number... Whatever is available, look for it and send it to me. And behold, the enemies oppress me but I shall not leave my wife and my children...before the enemy. And if the Hittites fall, I will send a message to you, and if they do not fall, I will certainly send a message... Our food in the threshing floors is sacked. And also the vineyards are destroyed. Our city is destroyed, and may you know it. – AMMURAPI, UGARIT TABLETS

way. However, the footsoldiers and their families were spared, many of them resettled in Egypt with land in frontier positions – barbarians rehoused with orders to block similar attacks from other barbarians.

The date of Ramses' battle against the Sea Peoples occurs about the same time as the devastating attacks on Mycenae and then Anatolia and Syria. As Ramses III himself reports, 'no country could stand before their arms.' Between 1200 and 1180, more places fell to the Sea Peoples: the palace of Mersin and city of Tarsus in Kode (Cilicia in southern Turkey); the kingdom of Arzawa (Turkey); the city of Carchemish in Syria, and the kingdom of Alashia in Cyprus.

Similar attacks are recorded in dramatic detail in clay tables written by King Ammurapi of Ugarit in Syria. These desperate pieces of correspondence report an overwhelming attack from 'seven ships'. That a whole city could be overrun by such a seemingly small number points to the fragility of civilizations in

ABOVE: The Phoenician
alphabet is shown here
on a terracotta tablet
dating from the fourteenth
century BCE.

the late Bronze Age. One well-timed attack could remove
an entire kingdom from the map.

Ammurapi's tablets provide an important picture of
greater unrest in the region than that caused by the Sea
Peoples. The tablets show that Ammurapi had also been
sending grain to Cilicia in Anatolia after the city had
suffered from poor harvests and subsequent famine. The
distribution of aid had been going on for some decades;
Pharaoh Merneptah had also supplied grain to the
Hittites to 'keep alive the land of Hatti'.

Modern climatologists have shown there was large-
scale drought across Anatolia and the Aegean at that time
– Hatti and Mycenae both suffered from these events. We
are reminded of the classical Greek historian Herodotus,
who speaks of pestilence, plague and famine in Crete
following the Trojan War, which rendered the island all
but uninhabitable.

Depopulation followed, both around Messenia and
central Anatolia. These clues suggest a great exodus
of people occurred as drought, famine, pestilence and
violence led them to pack up and search for somewhere
new to settle. The Sea Peoples, or other groups of
marauding barbarians – perhaps including Thracians,
Dorians, Luwians and even Mycenaeans – certainly took
advantage of these weakened international systems to
attack increasingly vulnerable city-states.

The end for the great superpowers of the Near East
and Mediterranean, who had proudly corresponded with the
other leaders of great civilizations as their 'brothers', was
desperate and terrible. Hattusa, the grand capital of the Hittites,
who had challenged the might of Egypt and carefully recorded
its diplomatic correspondence on thousands of cuneiform tablets,
was utterly destroyed around 1200 BCE. Before Hattusa's fall,
we see the familiar pattern of defensive works as employed by
the Mycenaean palaces: the construction of enormous cyclopean
walls and outlying forts as nervous correspondence calls for
warriors and information.

Suppiluliuma II, the last known king of Hatti, certainly ordered defensive works, but this building was to be in vain. When the end came, it was fast and brutal. The fire that engulfed the capital destroyed the palace and royal acropolis, the temples of the upper and lower cities, and the houses that lay below.

However, there was unlikely to have been a last stand at Hattusa; archaeological evidence shows that the city was abandoned before it was razed. Perhaps Suppiluliuma had read some hurried dispatches from the falling cities of Mycenae and ordered an evacuation of his capital. If this is correct, the king of one of the greatest empires of the Bronze Age followed a similar path to Aeneas and became the leader of an exiled, stateless people.

Year Zero in Greece

The Greek Dark Age cast Greece back to year zero: populations dwindled, towns became villages, the world shrank and became a closed, insular place. Centuries passed before civilization showed through the gloom; with it would come the new city-states of Greece and later the rise of the empires of Macedonia and Rome.

BELOW: The ruins that were once the Hattusa, capital of the great Hittite empire, are all that remain of the city.

Greece would quietly revive itself from the tenth century BCE, with a little help from the Phoenicians.

Settlements in places like Crete and Rhodes began to trade in emerging new crafts, such as pottery and jewellery. Over time, the Greeks set up trading networks from Syria in the east to Italy in the west; prosperity followed, as did an increase in population. By the eighth century, or around the time of Homer, Greece began its Archaic phase, the period between the Dark Age and Classical Greece in the fifth century BCE. During this time, Greek people moved away from their agricultural communities of the Dark Age and into cities – the *poleis*.

Archaic Greece lay the foundations for the Classical Age economically, culturally and politically. The Greek alphabet was developed during the Archaic period and used to record Homer's *Iliad*. Archaic Greece and the *Iliad* both presented the Greeks with an opportunity to think about the type of societies they wanted to create. Troy was always presented as the ordered, civilized city-state in contrast to the barbarity of the Mycenaean Greeks, who clashed egotistically with each other over leadership and loot. In many ways, Homer's portrait of the Mycenaeans was a portent and a warning of trouble ahead in Classical Greece.

Theirs was the chance not to repeat the mistakes of the Mycenaeans, a civilization led by nobles and kings who needed a steady supply of wealth to support their palatial lifestyles. In the *Iliad*, the undemocratic rule of kings is called into question by a footsoldier named Thersites, as the Greek coalition debates whether to continue the siege or return home.

Thersites is painted by Homer as the grotesque face of the malcontented Mycenaean proletariat and 'the ugliest man of all those that came before Troy – bandy-legged, lame of one foot, with his two shoulders rounded and hunched over his chest. His head ran up to a point, but there was little hair on the top of it.' But despite his unappealing countenance, the commoner Thersites has the courage to stand up to his social betters with

> Thersites is painted by Homer as the grotesque face of the malcontented Mycenaean proletariat and 'the ugliest man of all those that came before Troy'.

his squeaky voice, rather than accept whatever decision they are
ready to mete out.

'Agamemnon,' he cried, 'what ails you now, and what more
do you want? Your tents are filled with bronze and with fair
women, for whenever we take a town we give you the pick of
them. Would you have yet more gold, which some Trojan is to
give you as a ransom for his son, when I or another Achaean has
taken him prisoner? Or is it some young girl to hide and lie with?
It is not well that you, the ruler of the Achaeans, should bring
them into such misery. Weakling cowards, women rather than
men, let us sail home.' – HOMER, ILIAD, BOOK II

ABOVE: **A fragment of a
fifth century BCE Greek
manuscript of the Iliad,
written on parchment.**

Thersites is then sharply rebuked by Odysseus: 'Who are
you to wrangle with kings, you alone?' he demands, and beats
Thersites with a staff until the soldier weeps. It is a pivotal

HESIOD'S LAMENT

HESIOD WAS, AFTER HOMER, the great poet of the Archaic period and an outspoken commentator on the changing nature of society during the age of iron. In his *Works and Days*, Hesiod sings the praises of the rural life, the importance of hard toil in the fields and the corruption that will follow the Greeks into their new city lives. Hesiod bemoans the changing times and threatens divine punishment from Zeus for those who 'concern themselves with only outrageousness and wicked deeds.' Corruptible men only concerned with power and the accumulation of wealth will replace the honest and good, Hesiod continues, 'For now indeed it is a race of iron.' Hesiod uses the parable of the hawk and the nightingale to underline his lesson about the dangers of the polis:

And now I will tell a fable for princes who themselves understand. Thus said the hawk to the nightingale with speckled neck, while he carried her high up among the clouds, gripped fast in his talons, and she, pierced by his crooked talons, cried pitifully. To her he spoke disdainfully: 'Miserable thing, why do you cry out? One far stronger than you now holds you fast, and you must go wherever I take you, songstress as you are. And if I please I will make my meal of you, or let you go. He is a fool who tries to withstand the stronger, for he does not get the mastery and suffers pain besides his shame.' So said the swiftly flying hawk, the long-winged bird.

– HESIOD, *WORKS AND DAYS*

moment, one that is easily overlooked: in it the future destinies of Greece and Rome are laid out, for it is the clash between the rule of one strongman and a more democratic form of governance. Homer's poem had shown them the power and brutality of the heroic age, but also what happened when the destiny of the common man was left to the tyranny of kings.

The farming communities that had kept the population of Greece alive during its Dark Age were now splintering and an exodus began towards the new urban centres of the poleis. Tribal life gave way to a more sophisticated society; communal villages were abandoned for the promise of personal advancement and the possibility of private property. When Aristotle said man was a political animal, he meant man was a polis-dwelling creature.

The Polis

With the rise of the polis as the political centre, the age-old problem of the relationship between the elite few, known as *hoi oligoi*, versus the many, *hoi polloi*, came sharply into focus. Often a polis was founded by a charismatic strongman able to fend off neighbouring rivals. It is perhaps no surprise that Athens chose Theseus, the mythical hero and slayer of the minotaur, as its founding king.

Like the Mycenaean city-states that came before them, the Greek poleis were built in lofty, strategic positions that gave a commanding view of the surrounding agricultural land. Each polis had a highly fortified citadel at its highest point and populations ranging from 1000 to 10,000 inhabitants, in the

BELOW: Theseus, the mythical hero and slayer of the minotaur, here stands over his prize.

cases of the larger poleis such as Athens, Sparta, Corinth and Argos.

The polis, according to the philosopher Aristotle, represented the highest form of community, as public life was far more virtuous than the private life of the farmer or villager. In his *Politics*, or 'Things concerning the polis', Aristotle asserted that a citizen of the polis is 'Anyone that can take part in the city's governmental process'; most people, he added, are capable of this role. The polis, of course, was not only a place to trade, do business and be around others of the modern age, but also to become a politician.

While the great philosophers of Classical Greece argued about the freedom of man and the role of rulers and governments, there was little agreement about how this should work in practice during the Archaic Age. By the eighth century BCE, most poleis had abandoned kings as rulers and instead adopted some other form of government. Often these were run by oligarchs – rich elites who took on the individual public offices that would have previously been overseen by just one man, the king.

While the oligarchs of the poleis tended to monopolize positions of authority, it was possible for those from the lower orders to rise. Oligarchs had to deliver or suffer an uprising. In Argos in 370 BCE, a mob of dissatisfied commoners clubbed their aristocratic rulers to death and then turned on their own democratic leaders – the people had a voice and they would not suffer the rule of omnipotent kings as their Mycenaean ancestors had so often done.

BELOW: This bronze helmet is from Greece's Classical period.

The Introduction of the Hoplite

The introduction of iron weaponry and new techniques of fighting strengthened the ideals of equality for all poleis. At the centre was the hoplite soldier, literally a citizen soldier, who would fight alongside his comrades in a tight formation called a phalanx. With shields overlapping, a phalanx would move carefully forwards as a unit, crushing the opposition and thrusting their spears through the small gaps made in the shield wall. It was a formidably effective tactic, quickly employed by all of the Greek city-states and later imitated by the Roman army.

The hoplite soldier was very different from the aristocratic, imperious warrior-hero such as Achilles, although Achilles certainly remained their benchmark for bravery. With hoplites available, a city-state did not need to pay for a standing army or employ mercenaries in its wars against neighbouring city-states. Hoplites developed a fierce devotion to a particular polis, a place with its own distinct identity that also defined its members; dying for one's polis became a matter of duty.

The rise of the hoplite soldier also levelled the social playing field in Greece, as Aristotle himself noted: 'The class that does the fighting wields the power.' Alexander the Great and Julius Caesar would later be great advocates of this simple philosophy.

The City-State

Greek city-states had become strongly individualized by the Classical Age. Often a city-state defined itself by what it was not – Athens, for example, was not Sparta. Political identities also took different paths:

BELOW: An illustration of a hoplite from the Peloponnesian War.

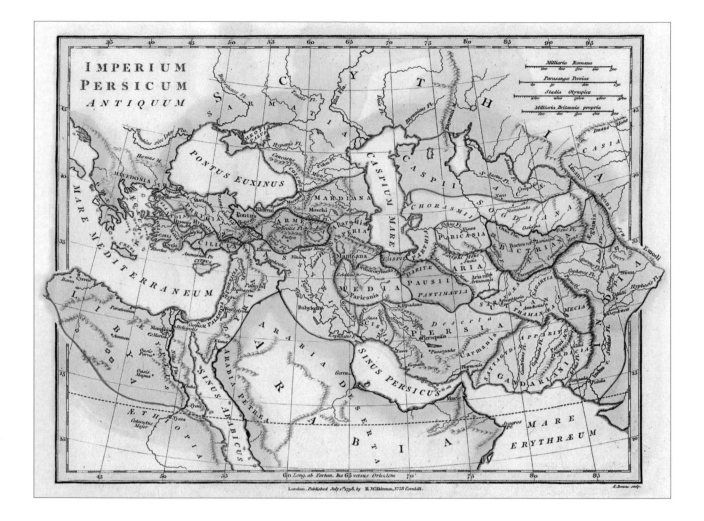

ABOVE: This map shows the boundaries of the Persian Empire in the fourth century BCE, just before it was crushed and conquered by Alexander the Great.

Sparta was ruled by two kings, a council of elders, and a public assembly, which rarely found common agreement; Athens famously invented rule of the male majority, an early form of democracy. Sparta prided itself on austerity and the tough life of its warrior citizens; weak baby boys would be killed at birth and the others sent off to train from the age of seven. Athens, by comparison, fostered a grand tradition of philosophy, art and literature; many of its citizens would become rich through trade and private enterprise.

Plato noted that Greek city-states would war against each other rather than seek out a peaceful coexistence: 'For "peace", as the term is commonly employed, is nothing more than a name, the truth being that every State is, by a law of nature, engaged perpetually in a war with every other State.' For a city-state such as Athens, Sparta was simply a rival; there was little reason to become friends. However, at one time the threat from an external enemy encouraged the Greeks to unite.

As Greece emerged from the Dark Age, empires to the east – where the Hittites once ruled – had come and gone. But every one of them – the Assyrians, Babylonians and Medes – would be eclipsed by the Persians. By 500 BCE, the Persian Empire stretched over nearly 15 million square kilometres (6 million square miles) and three continents and was the largest empire in the world. It would be only a matter of time before it set its sights on its Greek neighbours to the west.

The story of the epic struggle between Greece and Persia began in 499 BCE and would pit the famous Persian kings Darius and Xerxes against the Greeks. The Greeks united against the Persians for the first and only time in their ancient history. The details of the battles from this time ring out loud: the 300 Spartans at the pass of Thermopylae, the sea battle at Salamis, the sacking and burning of Athens. In the end, the Greeks were victorious against the Persians; their unity, however, would not last.

Philhellenes, or lovers of all things Greek, are often puzzled by the Classical Greeks' inability to form a political and economic union after their victories against the Persians. Instead, the Delian League, formed as an alliance of Greek city-states against the Persians, was to be their undoing. The members of the league had agreed to pay regular monies to Athens as a defence purse against future hostilities from outside. However, this only served to create hostilities from within, as Athens became ever more rich and powerful.

Soon, Athens took up a role as the police force of Greece: new colonies and garrisons

BELOW: A student of Socrates' and teacher of Aristotle, Plato was the unrivalled philosopher of Classical Greece.

were strategically placed around the Greek islands; violence was employed when city-states of the league were perceived to have stepped out of line. Sparta felt threatened by the rising star of Athens and became increasingly paranoid about its own security. A major conflict between the city-states, known to posterity as the Peloponnesian War, became inevitable.

In the end, the war lasted for over sixty years, engulfed every city-state in Greece, and all but destroyed them. It finished Greece's Golden Age and the great political experiments of its disparate members. After this devastation, a Macedonian strongman marched in to unite Greece and turn it into an empire; he is known to history as Alexander the Great.

Enter Aeneas' Rome
In his vision of himself as the great Achilles of Homer's *Iliad*, Alexander succeeded in the unification and expansion of Greece as a military empire. The Romans were the grand

BELOW: The 480 BCE Battle of Salamis pitched the formidable Greek fleet against that of the Persians. The Greek victory was recorded as history's first great naval battle.

ALEXANDER AND ACHILLES

Born of King Philip II of Macedon, Alexander was raised in what the Greeks considered the barbaric, backward Greek north, far from the civilized modern centres of Athens, Sparta and Corinth. For an urbanized Greek from the Classical Age, visiting Macedonia would have been like venturing back in time, to the period of warrior kings described in the *Iliad*. This was because the literature and traditions of Greece had been adopted by the Macedonians, but its politics had not. The Macedonians were instead made up of tribes and ruled by autocrats; they were skilled horse-riders, hunters and warriors, just as the Mycenaeans had been. It is little wonder that the character of Achilles resonated deeply with Alexander. Alexander's love for the *Iliad* was such that his famous tutor, Aristotle, prepared a copy of the poem that he kept under his pillow.

The *Iliad* served as a personal guide for young Alexander, who died at 32 after invading the Persian Empire and conquering a vast swathe of land stretching from Turkey to Iraq. As he disembarked from his ship in the Dardanelles, Alexander made sure he was the first to thrust a spear into Asian soil, just as the Greek Protesilaus had done at Troy. He also made a point of visiting the supposed tomb of Achilles:

Once arrived in Asia, he [Alexander] went up to Troy, sacrificed to Athena and poured libations to the heroes of the Greek army…he also remarked that Achilles was

Alexander is shown here with his beloved Hephaestion.

happy in having found a faithful friend while he lived and a great poet to sing of his deeds after his death.

– PLUTARCH, *PLUTARCH'S LIVES*

The 'friend' Plutarch mentions was, of course, Patroclus, who many believe had the same homosexual relationship that Alexander had with his constant companion, Hephaestion. Alexander never recovered from Hephaestion's death and died soon afterwards in 323 BCE.

ABOVE: Alexander the Great here visits the alleged tomb of Achilles.

masters of rule through dictatorship. The Romans traditionally acknowledged Greek superiority in art, literature and philosophy, but in other areas Rome considered itself more than Greece's equal. Devotion to the nation of Rome was an essential element of the Roman ideal of 'pietas', or a sense of duty to family, country and the gods.

The living embodiment of pietas was Aeneas, the founder of Rome, according to Virgil. In the *Aeneid*, the term 'pious Aeneas' is repeated 20 times. Aeneas is described as fiercely devoted to his people, swearing to take up 'combat once again' on their behalf after the sack of Troy or 'die this day unavenged'. Virgil portrayed Aeneas as a hero of discipline and patriotic devotion. He was a leader who would lead Rome to greatness – the founder of a city with a mission to rule the world. Virgil's great poem also provided an ideological charter for the Roman Empire under his patron Augustus.

Virgil's poem uses the theme of Troy and constantly recalls the Greek epic, even down to detailed echoes of Homer's words, but for a profoundly Roman purpose. It wholly fitted this purpose that Aeneas, the founder of Rome, was the survivor of the Greek holocaust at Troy. The Romans tended to view the Trojans as the civilized counterpoint to the barbaric Mycenaeans. It is unclear exactly when this became an issue of public policy, but the sentiment grew strong in 280 BCE, when Pyrrhus of Epirus – second cousin to Alexander the Great, who claimed lineage to Achilles – invaded the Italian mainland and referred to Rome as another Troy in waiting.

Armed with war elephants provided by Ptolemy II of Egypt, Pyrrhus sought to found an empire to match that of his cousin Alexander. He was also a skilled general; Hannibal, the famous

BELOW: **Pyrrhus' victory at the 279 BCE Battle of Asculum cost him 3,500 of his best troops.**

Carthaginian general who also attacked Rome with war elephants, considered him the greatest military mind of the age after Alexander.

Like Hannibal, Pyrrhus quickly proved himself capable of challenging the might of Rome, winning several victories against their legionaries on the Italian mainland. However, the Romans fought back strongly and although Pyrrhus continued to win battles he also sustained heavy losses (hence the term a 'Pyrrhic victory'). After losing 3500 of his crack troops to 6000 Roman legionaries at the 279 BCE Battle of Asculum, Pyrrhus famously commented that: 'If we are victorious in one more battle with the Romans, we shall be utterly ruined.'

BELOW: This marble bust shows the general known as Pyrrhus of Epirus, supposedly a direct descendent of Achilles.

In the end, Pyrrhus would be ousted from Italy and his services sought by the Sicilians, who needed a strong military man to defeat the Carthaginians occupying the west of their island. But after becoming King of Sicily, Pyrrhus so upset its inhabitants that they ended up making a pact with the Carthaginians themselves; Pyrrhus had no choice but to sail back to Greece.

The Romans of the Republican Age in 279 BCE did not yet know about Hannibal, but in a little over 60 years, the most dangerous Carthaginian of all would famously cross the Alps and invade much of Roman Italy. Like Pyrrhus before him, Hannibal would be defeated, but the Carthaginians would never be forgotten, nor forgiven.

Carthage became the Roman Republic's greatest enemy, bitterly hated by patricians and plebeians alike. The senator and orator Cato would famously end every one of his speeches with 'delenda est Carthago': 'Carthage must be

destroyed'. This moment would come, with great fury and
vengeance, in 146 BCE, the year when Rome both destroyed
Carthage and the Greek city-state of Corinth. It was the
year Rome established itself as the great superpower of the
Mediterranean, or 'Mare Nostrum' ('Our Sea'), as they called it.

However, the terror of Hannibal and Carthage was still fresh
in Roman minds when they first encountered Virgil's *Aeneid*
during the time of Augustus. Many readers would have been
instantly reminded of Hannibal when Queen Dido promised
untold strife between her kingdom and that of Aeneas, and calls
for 'someone to avenge me' after the Trojan rejects her. The
reference is one of many that linked Aeneas with the story of
Rome, and more importantly Augustus himself, who brought
about the Pax Romana after decades of terror and tyrannical rule
by Rome's warring generals.

Virgil read some of the books of the *Aeneid* to Augustus and
his wife Octavia as he was writing them; he intended to visit
Greece in 19 BCE to finish the epic but died before the poem

ABOVE: **Pyrrhus is shown
here centre stage at the
Battle of Beneventum.
It was a victory for the
Roman legionaries led
by consul Manius
Curius Dentatus.**

ABOVE: The Roman poet Virgil here reads his latest *Aeneid* chapters to Augustus, alongside his sister Octavia and wife Livia.

could be polished to his satisfaction. Virgil's will insisted the manuscript be destroyed if the poet died before it was published, but this dying wish was blocked by Augustus, who deemed the work too important to the Roman legacy, and most importantly his own.

Using the characters from Homer, the *Aeneid* was the Roman *Iliad* and *Odyssey* combined. Aeneas is destined to build the settlement by the Tiber that will later turn into the city of Rome; he was also supposedly the blood ancestor of Romulus and Remus through their mother Rhea Silvia, making the Roman people the Trojan's progeny.

It is no accident that the noble virtues Virgil portrayed in Aeneas, Rome's founder, are also those he hoped to encourage in its re-founder Augustus – at the time, Rome's best new hope of restoring peace and order. Aeneas' pietas could be taken either as a reflection or a guide to Augustus. There are certainly moments when the poet appears to speak directly to the *Princeps*, or 'First Citizen of Rome', as Augustus had cleverly called himself in lieu of 'Emperor'. One of these moments is when Aeneas is demonstrating his filial pietas by visiting his father Anchises in the underworld.

Here, Anchises reveals Aeneas' fate as the founder of Rome and warns of the good and bad leaders who will follow him. In a speech that can be taken as an address directly to Augustus, Anchises reminds Aeneas of the importance of pietas in the new people of Rome: 'Roman, remember by your strength to rule Earth's people – for your arts are to be these: To pacify, to impose the rule of law, To spare the conquered, to battle down the proud.'

> It is no accident that the noble virtues Virgil portrayed in Aeneas, Rome's founder, are also those he hoped to encourage in its re-founder, Augustus.

Roman Glory

Anchises describes the great glory that Augustus will bring to Rome: 'This is the man, this one, of whom so often you have heard the promise, Caesar Augustus, son of the deified, who shall bring once again an Age of Gold, to Latium, to the land where Saturn reigned in early times.'

Augustus was to end the civil war between the slayers of Julius Caesar and his champions, the last of whom is Augustus. Anchises warns against the spectre of a return of war: 'you must not bind your hearts to that enormity of civil war, turning against your country's very heart.' Instead it is for Augustus to rule over Rome as a patron of peace.

Augustus' Pax Romana was profoundly welcome after decades of slaughter by warring warlords. The brutal power struggle between Caesar and Pompey was only the last of these. Some Roman politicians, such as Cicero, had hoped for a return to the virtues of the Republic and a more democratic rule under the senate. However, all his rivals succeeded in doing was cutting down Rome's most successful strongman on the senate floor.

The rule of virtue had always been rare in Rome, and the murder of Julius Caesar would make its reappearance even more unlikely. The cycle of violence instead continued even more strongly. Caesar's killers had sounded the death knell for the Republic through the dictator's assassination; his heir Augustus, the eventual victor in the wars that followed Caesar's death, brought only a temporary period of peace.

The rulers who followed Augustus made the term 'Roman Emperor' a byword for decadence, depravity, megalomania and madness. Tiberius, Caligula and Nero showed themselves as the antithesis of Aeneas: the Trojan prince demonstrated his filial piety by carrying his father on his back from the burning city; Nero had his mother Agrippina murdered.

BELOW: The corpse of Caesar lies covered in his toga as the triumphant assassins celebrate, in this Jean-Leon Gerome painting.

In the end, Rome would fall to the sack of barbarians, just as Troy had. The empire had not lived up to the virtues preached by its founding father Aeneas, but instead became bloated, corrupt and ultimately unsustainable. However, for a few moments during the time of Augustus the idealist Virgil prays that Aeneas' Rome will live up to the promise of a virtuous future as offered to it by Aeneas:

Gods of our fathers, of our country, and Romulus, and Vesta, mother who keeps Tuscan Tiber and the Roman Palatine, forbid not this our prince from saving a ruined world. Long enough already has our life-blood recompensed Laomedon's perjury

ABOVE: **Nero here stands by his dead mother, the woman who he finally managed to murder after several failed attempts.**

at Troy; long already the heavenly palace, O Caesar, grudges thee to us, and murmurs that you should care for human triumphs, where right and wrong are confounded, where all these wars cover the world, where wickedness is so manifold and the plough's honour is gone; the fields thicken with weeds, for the tillers are marched away, and bent sickles are forged into the stiff swordblade: here the Euphrates, there Germany heaves with war; neighbouring cities rush into arms one against another over broken laws: the merciless War-God rages through all the world.

— VIRGIL, *GEORGICS*

Future Influence

Rome was sacked by the Visigoth hoards in the fifth century CE, but the Trojan myth continued even after the real centre of its power had moved from Rome to the eastern half of the empire and its capital in Constantinople. Constantine the Great, the first Christian emperor, had supposedly wanted to build his new capital at Troy, but was persuaded not to, partly because the harbour had long since silted over.

The Romans were not the only ones to proclaim themselves the descendants of the Trojans: many Western nations have claimed Troy as part of their founding myths. Even the Goths did so. According to Cassiodorus's 551 CE *History of the Goths*, the Ostrogoth Theodoric, now king of Italy, claimed to have Trojan blood as a way of legitimizing his rule on the old Roman mainland.

The Franks also claimed that their mythical founder was Francus the Trojan – Francus being a derivation of Astyanax, son of Hector. The Vikings too, according to the Icelandic sagas, had Trojan blood surging through their veins. This was because, according to saga author Snorri Sturluson, the Trojan warrior Menon had fathered a baby with Priam's daughter who was named Tror. It was this Tror, Snorri said, that 'We call Thor', the Norse god.

The royal Trojan line continued in Britain, the country raided and invaded by the Vikings. Here, *Historia Brittonum*, the tenth-century work of Welsh monk Nennius, described how Britain was settled by expatriates from Troy. The country had even apparently taken the name Britain from Brutus, a relation of Aeneas'. The story gained further appeal when retold by the twelfth-century cleric Geoffrey of Monmouth.

Monmouth's *History of the Kings of Britain* further embellished the story of Britain's founder, Brutus, adding that he was banished from Italy after killing his parents and then set sail to found new lands. On his journey, Brutus rescues a group of Trojans held captive in Greece before stumbling on more Trojan exiles, led by the warrior Corineus.

BELOW: This rendering of the fall of Rome shows the remains of the sacked city.

After fighting the Gauls, Brutus and Corineus sail to Britain, then called Albion, where they defeat the indigenous giants and Corineus becomes ruler of Cornwall. Brutus then travels east to found a city on the banks of the River Thames, which he names Troia Nova, or New Troy. In time, this becomes Trinovantum, and later London.

Geoffrey of Monmouth's work was of course historical fantasy, but the Tudor kings claimed it as proof of their Trojan heritage. Such was the prestige of the Trojan story that more than 2000 years later it could be invoked by rulers for political purposes. Elizabeth I became not only the direct descendant of Aeneas but also the representation of the 'Justice' that Virgil's *Eclogues* had said had fled the earth at the beginning of the Iron Age. Now, this 'Justice' had retuned as the virgin Queen, the bringer of Britain's Golden Age.

This was told to Elizabeth herself in Thomas Hughes' 1588 tragedy *The Misfortunes of Arthur*, performed before the monarch

BELOW: Ostrogoth king Theodoric the Great is shown here entering Rome. By 493 CE, Theodoric had conquered most of Italy.

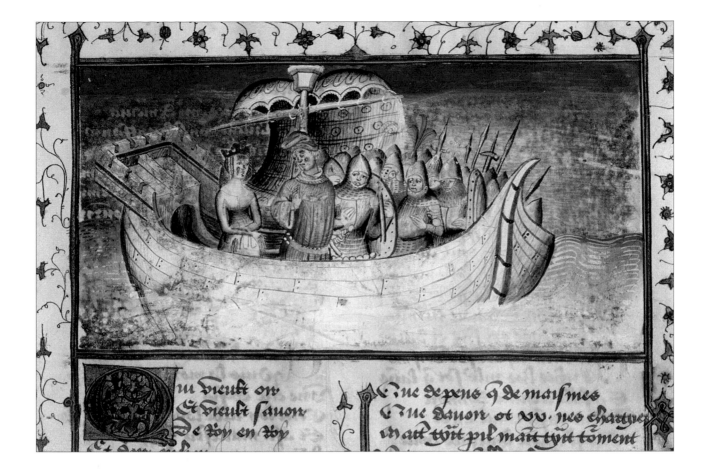

in Greenwich. The play praised Elizabeth as 'that virtuous Virgo born for Britain's bliss / That peerless branch of Brute: that sweet remain / Of Priam's state: that hope of springing Troy.'

Hughes' play reflected a British fascination with Troy in the sixteenth century; it was not only in vogue but provided source material for new stories. In Spenser's 1590 *Faerie Queen*, King Arthur is told of his Trojan lineage and Britomart finds out she is related to Brutus. Spenser, however, later admitted that 'it was impossible to prove that there was ever such Brutus of England.'

In the late sixteenth century, Christopher Marlowe's *The Tragedy of Dido, Queen of Carthage* and later *The Tragical History of Doctor Faustus* are both about Helen of Troy. Philip Henslowe mentions a production called *The Conquest of Brute with the First Founding of Bath*, which was staged at London's Rose Repertory. Across town at the Globe, Shakespeare had also taken up the topic of Troy. The Bard's *King Lear* and *Cymbeline* are about the kings of Britain following Brutus; *Troilus and*

ABOVE: Brutus the Trojan is shown here sailing to found a new Troy in Geoffrey of Monmouth's *The History of the Kings of Britain*.

AENEAS TO ARTHUR

In this 1475 painting, the Arthurian knights experience a vision of the Holy Grail at their Round Table.

GEOFFREY OF MONMOUTH'S *HISTORY of the Kings of Britain* says the British king, Arthur, is also the progeny of the Trojan Aeneas. This is repeated in the chivalric fourteenth-century poem *Sir Gawain and Green Knight*, perhaps the most famous story attached to Arthurian legend:

After the siege and the assault of Troy, when that burg was destroyed and burnt to ashes, and the traitor tried for his treason, the noble Aeneas and his kin sailed forth to become princes and patrons of well-nigh all the Western Isles. Thus Romulus built Rome (and gave to the city his own name, *which it bears even to this day); and Ticius turned him to Tuscany; and Langobard raised him up dwellings in Lombardy; and Felix Brutus sailed far over the French flood, and founded the kingdom of Britain, wherein have been war and waste and wonder, and bliss and bale, oft times since. And in that kingdom of Britain have been wrought more gallant deeds than in any other; but of all British kings Arthur was the most valiant, as I have heard tell, therefore will I set forth a wondrous adventure that fell out in his time.*

— SIR GAWAIN AND THE GREEN KNIGHT

Cressida is based on the *Iliad*; and *Henry V* has the immortal line spoken by Pistol to Fluellen: 'Base Trojan, thou shalt die.'

In modern times, this reference seems obscure, but in the sixteenth century, Shakespeare could assume that every member of the audience would understand its reference to Troy.

The interest in Troy during the Tudor period helped spark new translations of the *Iliad*, a trend that began in the sixteenth century and continues to the present day. Among the most famous early versions are those by George Chapman and in the eighteenth century by Alexander Pope. Chapman was promised £300 by his patron Prince Henry to finish the poem, but died before settling the fee. Pope fared rather better financially, and was paid two hundred guineas to translate the *Iliad*, a grand sum. Although in the end Pope only translated some of the *Iliad* and enlisted William Broome and Elijah Fenton to help with the rest, he became fantastically wealthy through his book sales. Today, first editions of Chapman and Pope's *Iliad* sell for tens of thousands of pounds.

BELOW: **An image from Shakespeare's *Troilus and Cressida*, which is based on the *Iliad*.**

New translations of the *Iliad* into English continue: Richard Lattimore, Robert Fitzgerald, Robert Fagles and Barry B. Powell's are among the most popular. Homer is still big business. It is a sign of Troy's reach that the poems from antiquity – The *Iliad*, *Odyssey* and *Aeneid* – still sell millions of units for publishing houses producing new translations. The ancient siege and sack of Troy are still part of our literary and cultural DNA.

The Modern View

Today, whole academic departments devote themselves to Homer and Virgil's texts; others explore the archaeological sites of Mycenae, Troy and Hatti.

Countless books about Troy have been written, including fiction, graphic novels and historical romance as well as non-fiction. There are many references to Troy in popular culture. Songs have included Bob Dylan's 'Temporary Like Achilles' and Led Zeppelin's 'Achilles' Last Stand'; synthpop band Crüxshadows wrote a whole album about Troy.

Television too has found ways of taking advantage of the enduring popularity of Troy: Doctor Who once popped up at Troy in his TARDIS, suggesting the idea of the wooden horse to the Greeks; Xena, Warrior Princess travelled to Troy to help her 'friend' Helen. The 2017 miniseries *Troy: Fall of a City* told the story in eight episodes; an earlier miniseries, *Helen of Troy*, hit the screens in 2003.

A common complaint from scholars and lovers of the legend of Troy is the vast number of historical inaccuracies that accompany screen adaptations of Troy. Television's *Helen of Troy*, for example, set the action in Classical Greece instead of the Bronze Age and was made quickly to ride on the coat-tails

BELOW: Part of Alexander Pope's translation of Homer's *Iliad*, shown here scrawled on a postcard for posterity.

of the 2004 film epic, *Troy*. Inspired by the *Iliad* itself, *Troy* sacrificed attempts to remain true to Homer, or historical accuracy, when these got in the way of its moviemaking. The gods do not feature in the movie at all; Menelaus and Agamemnon are killed off; and Peruvian llamas are shown wandering through the marketplace.

It is easy to ridicule modern attempts to recreate the tale of Troy, especially when created by Hollywood. However, they are part of the story's 2800-year-old tradition, in all of its forms. Troy has been massaged, bent out of shape and occasionally brutally misrepresented, but the tale will not die, despite its endless manhandling. Some of the most memorable reimaginings of the story, in fact, are those that depart most boldly from the Homeric text.

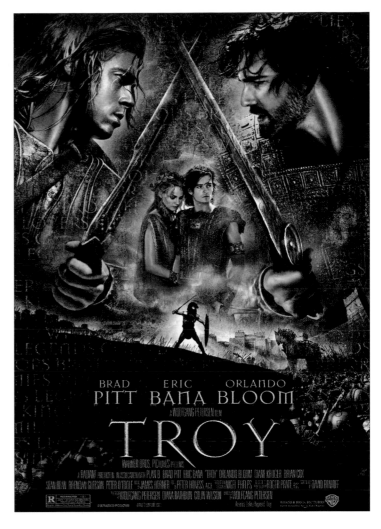

ABOVE: A poster for *Troy*. In the movie, new motifs such as the 'Sword of Troy' are sewn arbitrarily into the story's fabric.

A modern and fragmentary version of the *Iliad* by British poet Christopher Logue, for instance, upset purists by its deliberately anachronistic metaphors and its eccentric use of language. Logue's Homer pillages the lexicon of an extraordinary range of modern English, including that of advertising slogans – he uses a lipstick slogan, 'all day permanent red', to describe the gore of battle. Yet the power of Logue's *Iliad* is undeniable and the poet is surely right when he says that the translation of Homer's great poem must itself be a great poem.

Homer continues to inspire great poems just as it spawns bad and popular films and mediocre stagings. But whatever the results, the *Iliad* still refuses to release us from its grip. The light from Achilles' helmet, as Logue puts it, still 'screams across 3000 years'.

MAP OF BRONZE AGE GREECE

THIS MAP SHOWS THE late Bronze Age Aegean Sea and western Anatolia around 1250 BCE. The major Mycenaean city-states of Pylos, Sparta, Tyrins and Mycenae formed a ring around the central plain of Argos on Greece's Peloponnese. The royal palaces of these city-states needed great wealth to support themselves, and sacking cities around the Aegean was a way of generating revenue. The city of Troy was a rich and perhaps irresistible prize, perched on the northwest corner of Anatolia, today's Turkey. Here, at the southern entrance to the Dardanelles, a narrow straight that links the Black and Aegean Seas, 1,000 Mycenaean ships were said to have landed at a beach below Troy.

For 10 years, the Mycenaeans supposedly encamped and laid siege to the city. However, according to legend, only an act of trickery would allow the warriors to overcome the great walls of Troy.

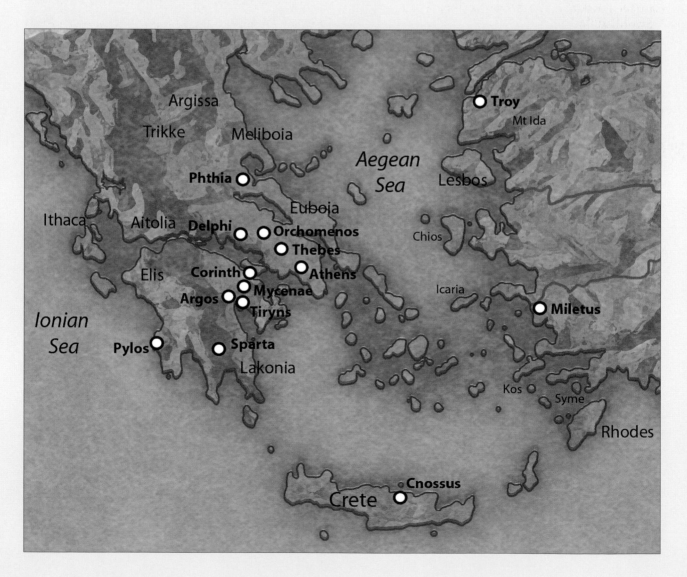

BIBLIOGRAPHY

Alexander, Caroline. *The War that hilles: The True Story of Homer's Iliad and the Trojan War* (Viking, 2009)

Allen, Susan Heuck. *Finding the Walls of Troy: Frank Calvert and Heinrich Schliemann at Hisarlik* (University of California Press, 1999)

Blegen, Carl W. *Troy and the Trojans* (Praegar, 1963)

Bryce, Trevor. *Life and Society in the Hittite World* (Oxford University Press, 2004)

Burkett, Walter. *Greek Religion* (Basil Blackwell, 1985)

Cantarell, Eva. *Bisexuality in the Ancient World* (Yale University, 2002)

Carol G. Thomas and Craig Conant. *The Trojan War* (University of Oklahoma Press, 2005)

Castleden, Rodney. *The Attack on Tory* (Pen & Sword, 2006)

Cook, J. M. *The Troad: An Archeological and Topographical Study* (Clarendon Press, 1973)

Chadwick, John. *The Mycenaean World* (Cambridge University Press, 1976)

Dickinson, Oliver T. P. K. *The Aegean Bronze Age* (Cambridge University Press, 1994)

Finley, Moses I. *The World of Odysseus* (Penguin, 1956)

Fields, Nic. *Mycenaean Citadels C. 1350–1200 BC* (Osprey, 2004)

Graves, Robert. *The Siege and Fall of Troy* (The Folio Society, 2005)

Griffin, Jasper. *Homer on Life and Death* (Oxford University Press, 1983)

Gurney, O. *The Hittites*, (Penguin, 1973)

Hanson, Victor Davis. *The Western Way of War: Infantry Battle in Classical Greece* (University of California Press, 1989)

Homer. *Iliad*, translations by Butler, Samuel (Theophania Publishing, 2011); Fagles, Robert (Penguin, 1990); Fitzgerald, Richard (OUP, 1984); Lattimore, Richard (Routledge, 1951); Pope, Alexander (Ulan Press, 2012)

Homer. *Odyssey*, translations by Butler, Samuel (CreateSpace, 2017); Fitzgerald, Robert (Random House, 1961); Lattimore, Richard (Bristol Classical Press, 1991)

Hughes, Bettany. *Helen of Troy: Goddess, Princess* (Jonathan Cape, 2005)

Kirk, G. S. *Homer and the Oral Tradition* (Cambridge University Press, 2010)

Latacaz, Joachim. *Troy and Homer: Towards a Solution of an Old Mystery* (Oxford University Press, 2004)

Lloyd, Alan B. (ed.). *Battle in Antiquity* (Gerald Duckworth & Co, 1996)

Luce, J. V. *Celebrating Homer's Landscapes: Troy and Ithaca Revisited* (Yale University Press, 1999)

Logue, Christopher. *War Music: An Account of Homer's Iliad* (Faber & Faber, 2017)

Morris, Ian (ed.). *The Dark Ages of Greece* (Edinburgh University Press, 1 July 2009)

Nagy, Gregory. *The Best of Achaeans: Concepts of the Hero in Archaic Greek Poetry* (The Johns Hopkins University Press, 1998)

Nicolson, Adam. *The Mighty Dead, Why Homer Matters* (William Collins, 2014)

Oswald, Alice. *Memorial: An Excavation of the Iliad* (Faber & Faber, 2012)

Redfield, James M. *Nature and Culture in the Iliad: The Tragedy of Hector* (Duke University Press Books, 1994)

Sanders, Nancy. *The Sea Peoples: Warriors of the Ancient Mediterranean, 1250–1150 BC* (Thames and Hudson, 1985)

Schein, Seth L. *The Mortal Hero: An Introduction to Homer's Iliad* (University of California Press, 1985)

Schofield, Louise. *The Mycenaeans* (J. Paul Getty Trust Publications, 2007)

Slatkin, Laura M. *The Power of Thetis: Allusion and Interpretation in the Iliad* (University of California Press, 1991)

Strauss, Barry. *The Trojan War: A New Story* (Arrow Books, 2008)

Trail, David A. *Schliemann of Troy: Treasure and Deceit* (St. Martin's Griffin, 1995)

Tsountas, Chrestos. *The Mycenaean Age, Study of the Monuments and Culture of Pre-Homeric Greece* (Kessinger, 2009)

Ventris, Michael. *Documents in Mycenaean Greek* (Cambridge University Press, 1976)

Virgil. *Aeneid*, translations by Fagles, Robert (Penguin, 2010); Fitzgerald, Robert (Penguin, 1983); Knight, Jackson W. F. (Penguin, 1956)

Wace, A. J. B. *Mycenae: an Archeological History and Guide* (Princeton University Press, 1949)

Wood, Michael. *In Search of the Trojan War* (BBC Books, 2008)

INDEX

Page references in *italics* refer to illustration captions.

PICTURE CREDITS